DISCARDED

SILVER RENAISSANCE

*Essays in Eighteenth-Century
English History*

EDITED BY

ALEX NATAN

Senior History Master at King's School, Worcester

LONDON
MACMILLAN & CO LTD
NEW YORK · ST MARTIN'S PRESS
1961

MACMILLAN AND COMPANY LIMITED
London Bombay Calcutta Madras Melbourne

THE MACMILLAN COMPANY OF CANADA LIMITED
Toronto

ST MARTIN'S PRESS INC
New York

PRINTED IN GREAT BRITAIN

Contents

Introduction

No interpretation of history which seeks to present the past as an example to be imitated or followed can be taken seriously. What has been and what is will never be again; the lessons of history must be looked for elsewhere. History is the result of Man's determination to carry on resolutely in the face of disaster, change and reconstruction, unless and until the obsessions of scientists and of suicidal politicians prevail. Wars, conquests, misery, famine, disorders of every kind, whether resulting from human errors or from natural calamities, may follow each other in quick succession; but they will never quench that inner flame which enables those who survive to persevere and to believe in progress. One lesson which history teaches us is never to despair.

The eighteenth century witnessed tremendous changes, fundamental turning-points for those who were the contemporaries of Locke, Burke and Thomas Paine, of Walpole and the Pitts, of Pope, Fielding and Wordsworth. Englishmen could bask in the golden sunset of the Augustan Age, and give free rein to their emotions with Romantic abandon. They may have sensed with some apprehension the implications of the Agrarian and Industrial Revolutions. When the Bastille fell, they may have mourned it as a symbol of the past, or hailed its capture as the harbinger of an exciting future. It remains the task of the historian to present the broad stream of events, to shed light on the less noticeable but often more significant changes which occurred under the shadow of transformation, and to show the interdependence of all the strands that weave the tapestry of English civilization.

It is the purpose of *Silver Renaissance* to arouse interest in those men who were not necessarily protagonists on the historical stage, and in those events which throw their own light on the brilliant spectacle of the eighteenth century. It is not a textbook, but a collection of essays which should rekindle interest in a century which may easily prove to have been a mellow age of human accomplishment.

ALEX NATAN

I

Dissent and Toleration

by J. STEVEN WATSON

WE are accustomed to think of the eighteenth century as a period of peace and tolerance. The seventeenth century in England had been a time of conflict, of confusion, and of coercion. With the opening of the nineteenth century men's minds appeared to become loftier but also narrower; great purposes were achieved only at the expense of ruthless rigidity. By contrast, the intervening century seems peaceful and relaxed, a valley of rough geniality and stagnation. Men then were too urbane to practise what the zealots preached, too lazy to enforce cruel laws: lacking belief, they could not be bigots. The lions of the establishment suffered the lambs of dissent to lie down quietly with them — at a proper distance. This is not the view of later generations only. Toleration was the feature of English life singled out for praise by Voltaire, a contemporary and a visitor. But how far do the facts support such generalizations?

Charles Wesley, in 1743, gives a description of the men of Sheffield which is reminiscent of the Ephesians of the first century. 'They pressed hard', he records, 'to break open the door (of the Methodist meeting house). . . . They laboured all night for their master (Satan) and by the morning had pulled down one end of the house. I could compare them to nothing but the men of Sodom, or those coming out of the tombs, exceeding fierce.' And by next day the enraged Yorkshiremen had left 'not one stone upon another' of the house in which men dared to preach an unusual holiness. The Methodists were not alone in suffering thus. In 1710 orthodox but frenzied Londoners had attempted the destruction of the halls of all those who would not conform to pattern. Nor was such intolerance the prerogative of Anglican crowds. Up in Edinburgh in 1779 the Presbyterian ruling class met the proposal to relieve Papists of a civil stigma with arson, pillage, and a flood of sermons all inciting to violence. In London the popular intolerance was slower to manifest itself but even more alarming in action. Sir George Savile's Acts which ameliorated the lot of Dissenters were passed; but they were followed by riots in which prisons were broken open, the streets ran with alcohol, and houses were smashed, while the civil power stood helplessly by. In that week in June 1780 Lord George Gordon's followers, howling for intolerance, were more completely masters of London than the devotees of liberty were of Paris in July 1789.

It was not religious questions alone which could rouse this passion of enraged conservatism. The men of Birmingham who wrecked Dr Priestley's house in 1791 resented his politics as much as his religion, and had even, perhaps, a superstitious dislike of his reputation for scientific exploration. Those who pelted to death men pilloried on charges of sexual abnormality were behaving with the automatic ferocity of the herd: upon such moods Burke's pleas for careful justice made no impression.

How then can these two pictures of the eighteenth century be reconciled? Or is it not a matter of reconciliation but of choosing between them? The easy answer would be that an urbane and civilized minority ruled over a population in which the conformist instincts of the herd broke out occasionally into violence. There is some truth in this. But it is not a sufficient answer. Why was there a rise in temperature among the ruling classes as well as the populace at the end of the century?

Between 1770 and 1780 men of liberal mind had begun to translate their principles into legal and administrative form. The Quebec Act of 1770 had allowed to Roman Catholics in Canada the rights of respectable citizens. In 1772 the Anglican clergy who met at the Feathers Tavern petitioned for a less rigid application of the Thirty-Nine Articles as a test of orthodoxy. The University of Cambridge began to admit undergraduates with less searching enquiry into their Anglican beliefs. The London Dissenters Committee took up with renewed hope its lobbying of ministers for the modification of the Test Act. In 1778 relief was proposed for both Protestant and Roman Catholic dissenters in Ireland. It was backed by arguments utilitarian as well as moral. For England at war with America, and menaced by France and Spain, could not afford Irish discontent. 'I think I should rather risk a Papist's purchasing an estate for himself', wrote Burke to the Speaker of the Irish House of Commons, 'than provoke him, and arm France, to deprive me of mine.'[1] He condemned the folly which kept thousands of men in discontented poverty by preventing Papists owning property, and all 'lest obnoxious people should in an hundred years creep by industry into a little better state'. On such grounds relief was given in Ireland and also in England.

But this gathering movement of toleration aroused the King, the squires, the bishops and the Scots: their hostility was communicated to the middle classes of London. The mobs gathered under respectable leaders. The key to this was fear. For, to quote Burke again (in a letter about Scotland to Dr Erskine written in 1779), 'I really believe these gentlemen are in earnest when they talk of self-

[1] 3rd July, 1778 (from a photostat in National Library of Ireland).

preservation — but fear which is always cruel, is not always founded. . . . Against enemies it is easy to believe any ill, and the rules of hostility admit of almost every sort of violence.' The reason therefore for the explosion of passion in 1780 was fear that 'the system' was being dismantled — a fear which was intensified after 1789 by a godless revolution in France. In defence of its system eighteenth-century England lost its tolerance, a tolerance which had always been limited and conditioned by the acceptance of a social and legal pattern.

It is a surprisingly common misconception that toleration was introduced by the Toleration Act of 1689. But that Act was limited, grudging, and opportunist. It consolidated the revolution of William and Mary. The Anglican interest had expelled James II and all his Popish absolutist ideas. In doing so it had had the support of the Protestant dissenters, whose own earlier rebellion had come to a sorry end at Sedgemoor under Monmouth. The new régime wished to make lasting the alliance against Romanism, and hoped to conciliate the Nonconformists without giving them any power. The Toleration Act therefore, without repealing the political or administrative sections of the Clarendon Code, allowed Protestant dissenters to register their meeting place and then (so long as the doors were not locked) to worship God in their own fashion. In return for loyalty to the new monarchy they were allowed to exist outside the Church of which that monarch was head. It was part of the plan that no benefit should accrue to Roman Catholics. On the contrary, the laws against them were tightened up. In the Act against Popery of 1700, for instance, Popish priests were threatened with life imprisonment for conducting a service, and informers were encouraged by the prospect of £100 for every conviction they brought about. In addition, Roman Catholics refusing the

Oaths of Allegiance and Supremacy were made incapable of inheriting landed property: Protestant members of their families were given the full use of such property. In other Acts special steps were taken to keep Papists out of London.

In the end the Tory reaction in Anne's reign made little difference to the picture. For most of the eighteenth century the legal position was quite clear. Protestant dissenters were allowed to practise their religion but were excluded from political life; their schoolmasters were supposed to obtain a licence and to attend the Anglican Church; they were occasionally harried by officious Anglican priests about baptism, marriage or burial, but their position was acknowledged and protected. Papists, on the other hand, were prevented from conducting schools, unable to inherit or purchase land when over eighteen, and liable to imprisonment for attending Mass. Proselytizing and conversion were held to amount to high treason. A convicted recusant could be banned from coming within ten miles of London, and limited to five miles' travel from his own home. Penalties for obstinate refusal to recognize the service of the Church of England could be gradually stepped-up from preventing the convicted man from having a house worth more than £5 to exile from England on the pain of a felon's death. An English-born Roman priest travelling abroad and then returning (for more than three days) was guilty of high treason.

As everyone knows, these fierce laws were not enforced. The victory of the Anglican squirearchy was seen to be secure once George I was on the throne. Fear either of Roman priests and French absolutism or of Cromwellian fighting democrats quietly died away, and with fear went the need to persecute. The landed gentry were content to hold the realities of power both at Westminster and at the quarter sessions in the counties. They had no wish to remodel England. They wished merely to run their own pieces of it. Respect for property was enough to secure their own predominance. They presented the Anglican parson to his living, and heard his sermons from their family pew; they expected every forelock to be touched respectfully to them whatever unruly thoughts might lurk behind it.

The Roman Church survived in England apparently only as a decaying curiosity. It was the religion of foreigners and eccentrics. When the lord of the manor happened, by family tradition, to be a Papist then his village might follow in his faith. There are examples of this all over the country. Up in Yorkshire, for instance, Viscount Fauconberg was surrounded not only by household servants, but by masons, farmers, butchers and so on who adhered with him to the Papacy. Mass might perhaps be said in the great house. But such communities lived an isolated existence. The Papist squire was permitted to protect his religion in the village, but he did not aspire to play a part in county affairs, much less in national ones. Only exceptionally would an informer attempt to break in upon the retired peace of such adherents to the old faith.

The Protestant dissenters were also cut off from a leading part in national politics, but their influence in the local government of the towns was not inconsiderable. It is at times difficult to decide whether they were really debarred from the House of Commons by their faith, or whether they held to this faith because they had a social position and a temperament which made them incapable of aspiring to go to Westminster. For, apart from Unitarians (who were excluded from the Toleration Act) and Quakers, much of the old fire seemed to have left the sects as it had been quenched in the Church. Enthusiasm, until the Wesleys and Whitefield revived it, was extinguished. So to dissent became almost a sign of faithfulness to a class rather than of cleaving to a faith. It was quite common for the successful son of a Dissenter to join the Anglican Communion once he had wealth enough to be ambitious of rising in the social scale. The Ryder family, for example, left the counter and the chapel at the same time to progress by way of the Bar and the Established Church right up to the House of Lords. Harley, Lord Oxford, was an earlier example of one who thought, unlike his ancestors, that a seat in Parliament was worth the Thirty-Nine Articles. To go to church became, in short, as it was long to remain, a sign of respectability or of social ambition.

The Nonconformists took part in local politics in spite of the laws intended to keep them out of every governing service. They profited by the absence of any strong or effective central authority. Groups of Dissenters were strong and unmolested in localities as far apart as Tiverton, Devon, or Sudbury, Suffolk. So far from harrying them, the Duke of Newcastle while at the Treasury instructed his prospective candidates for Parliamentary seats in Sussex to seek out and conciliate local leaders of Nonconformity.

It is usually said that the laws against Dissenters holding borough office were, in effect, suspended by the passage of an annual indemnity act. This is not strictly true. The practice of passing an indemnity act, to excuse offenders from immediate penalties under the 1673 Test Act, was not begun until 1728. Until then the battle between zealous Anglicans and latitudinarian Whigs had not been decided. From 1728 to 1757 there were seven years (or almost one in four) in which no indemnity acts were passed. From 1758 to 1828 the indemnity act became a regular event.

The years when no act was passed were years of particular strain or excitement, when country-gentlemen

M.Ps, the independent members, would not have permitted Ministers to slip in such an indulgence even at the
tail-end of a session. The threat of the Jacobite invasion,
for instance, was marked by a silent comment in the
Statute book, the absence of any indemnification of
offences under the Test Act. It did not follow that all such
offences were punished, of course. George III himself put
the position clearly. He argued in 1772, when the movement to amend the law relating to the Thirty-Nine
Articles seemed likely to lead on to a dismantling of
the Test Acts, that it was not only undesirable but un-
necessary to alter the status of Dissenters. 'It is the duty of
Ministers . . . to prevent any alteration in so essential a
part of the Constitution as everything that pertains to
religion, and there is no shadow for this petition, as the
Crown regularly grants a Nolle prosequi if any over-nice
Justice of Peace encourages prosecutions.' It was, in other
words, quite normal for the Crown to intervene by for-
bidding a prosecution to go forward (this is *nolle prosequi*)
even when an offence had been committed and when there
had not been any indemnification. The Acts against Protestants kept them in an inferior civic position: they were
further used at most to nag and worry but not to harry them.

Why then did the King regard the Acts as 'so essential a
part of the Constitution' — an opinion he shared with the
great majority of the landed gentry? The answer is obvious.
It was because in the static society of the century a conception of society almost Aristotelian had command of
men's minds. The state was a natural growth, like a household on a larger scale. In this natural partnership men
were unequal: so long as each knew his place and accepted
it, friendly and easy relations were possible. As in an
Aristotelian *polity*, there was a superior class which had a
chance of filling the great offices of state as full citizens:

below them the artisans led their own lives, debarred from administration but able occasionally to show general approbation of the way their betters were conducting affairs: lower still were beings who had no part but to work and to obey, supplying the necessities of life for those who were capable of living it fully. To be a Nonconformist was an acceptance of a category of second-class citizen. The way out of this inferiority was not quite closed to the enterprising individual: but it involved apprenticeship to a new way of life, of which the Anglican Church was a symbol. To propose to take away the signs of inferiority, however little they were punitive, was to initiate a new view of society, a levelling and a radical revolution. The whole pattern of England was involved in these restrictions. So deep was the conservatism of the century that the lower orders themselves could be easily aroused to defend the old distinctions; for mob action, too, had a recognized place in the eighteenth-century pattern of things.

As second-class citizens, then, the Protestant nonconformists built up a life and a culture of their own. Their importance depended not only upon their wealth. Debarred from the universities and kept out of many schools, they developed their own plan of education. The orthodox eighteenth-century education was based upon the literature of classical times. The dissenting academies, in contrast, laid less stress upon learning grammar and rather more upon useful subjects such as mathematics. At first sight this might appear to be more the education, in modern terms, of a secondary modern as opposed to a grammar school, but in time it acquired a life and force of its own. In mathematics, in the study of living languages, in political philosophy and economy, in the new study of the sciences, in all these the dissenting academies were often in advance of the established institutions. In the generation from 1730 to 1800 the Nonconformist intellectuals of England had a prominence out of proportion to their numbers. Men such as Priestley, Price, or Godwin could compete on equal terms with the Scots who for fifty years had been the masters of speculation.

Joseph Priestley may serve as an example of this flowering of Nonconformity. He was the son of a clothdresser, reared as a Calvinist, and polished in his young manhood at Daventry Academy under Caleb Ashworth. As a Presbyterian minister he found that his own arguments led him away from the fundamentalist creed of his congregation. Then, while tutor in languages at Warrington Academy, he embarked on theological paths which brought upon him charges of atheism. He became the protégé of Lord Shelburne, the source for one part of Bentham's utilitarianism, the discoverer of oxygen; he was finally so teased and tormented in England for his heresies that he emigrated to the United States. Richard Price was another product of this educational system, a leading theorist on fiscal questions, a radical in politics who defended the Americans and the French, believing that they shared his principles and democratic prejudices. William Godwin was the political writer who had perhaps the greatest influence upon rebellious young men at the very end of the century. His *Political Justice* is bloodless stuff, but to those of Shelley's generation it seemed the key to a new world. Godwin learned his philosophy at Hoxton Academy and became himself, before his atheist days, a dissenting minister. For vigour and originality what figures can be found to rival these on the side of the establishment? Learning and scholarship are to be found there, but little that is speculative. Erasmus Darwin perhaps, Jeremy Bentham certainly, may challenge the comparison. But Bentham turned his back upon his origins in Westminster

School and The Queen's College, Oxford, when he gave up the English bar. The development of his mind was such that he appears a Nonconformist by adoption: certainly his educational ideas, which eventually reached fruition in a university in London, owed much to the spirit of the dissenting academies.

There were defects in the culture of Nonconformity. Naturally enough the speculation of its leaders seemed abstract, lacking in realism, and tending to extremes. It is just such faults that Burke attacks in Tom Paine; and Paine with his Quaker background, his forty unsuccessful years in obscure jobs, his ambitions, and his clear commonsense, was yet another product of submerged but uncrushable English Nonconformity. The Nonconformist schools produced men who could look forward to jobs in business, or in lecturing and sermonizing. They were not bred to the responsibilities of power in Church and State. Their outlook was therefore, in respectable eyes, 'irresponsible'. But it was not incoherent.

Nonconformity, though it had apparently fallen asleep for half a century, had its roots in the seventeenth century. Its revolutionary aspect had not been entirely lost to sight. Quietly, in little-read books and papers, it had kept alive the ideas of the Cromwellians. It was this tradition, along with the rules of the faith, which gave coherence and training to its members, and prevented them from losing their self-respect and self-consciousness. They did not rot, as intelligent men without adequate opportunities often do: a code of morals, a past history, and theological puzzles to exercise the brain of an intelligent believer, preserved their vigour just as it preserved that of the Scots. So, at the end of the century, they were able to emerge from obscurity and to begin again their battle with the establishment.

So long as they were not missionaries they were tolerated as a peculiar but quiet people. They served a respectable purpose. In the ordinary English village the common man needed the squire and the parson to rule and guide him. They gave to life its serenity and such graces as it had. The Nonconformist chapel gave to some sections of the population, in the older towns, a similar sense of security. In areas such as the Somerset coalfield, or in Manchester, where the framework had collapsed, the poor were brutal, hopeless and purposeless. The older Nonconformist churches did not rush into the void to revive hope or to recruit adherents. Their sphere of operations was among the decent tradesmen and shopkeepers of the older towns. They were more like a friendly society, a club, or a religious debating society than a band of evangelists. Their radicalism had grown respectable simply by achieving a familiar place in the scheme of things. They did not envisage the possibility of seizing the leadership of those who had no known place in society: if they had, they would have rejected it. Their missionary activity was reserved for distant scenes, for India or America. They were in the grip of a social order so strong that they had ceased for a while to dream of smashing it.

It was the Methodists, slowly emerging from the bosom of the Anglican Church, who came forth to convert the English. They left the church in the market place and the tabernacle in the back street, and stood in the fields to preach to outcasts and restless men. Their aim was not political. It was to give hope to the lost and a sense of communion with God to those without friends. Because this enthusiastic campaign was strange it was resented. It was met with violence (such as that in Sheffield already described) because violence was natural to a society intolerant of change. In higher walks of life the weapons used were not stones but a smiling or a disgusted shrug of the shoulders. Lady Huntingdon, the patron of revivalism, was tolerated because of her social position but regarded as certainly eccentric and probably dangerous in her insistence that all men were sinners.

Yet Methodism was a preservative of the social order. The old Nonconformist churches were in protest against the hierarchical organization of England even if that protest was muted or had become a form of words only. The Methodists encouraged the most restless fringe of society to look up to heaven and to forget their grievances. In range, energy, and disregard of conventions they might seem to be a great popular movement, but the lesson they taught was tranquillizing. They did not encourage men to reform England but to rehabilitate themselves. If the soul was rendered unto God there was no point in quibbling about rendering everything else to Caesar or the squire.

When the Methodists eventually stepped outside the established Church this still remained true of them. It was not until the nineteenth century that the Wesleyan Church, by developing its own communal life, its sense of unity, and its training in self-government, acquired a radical tinge. The evangelical movement inside the Anglican Church was also conservative in this sense. By its gravity and restraint it avoided the hostility shown towards Wesley. It aimed at inculcating higher standards of behaviour among the powerful and bringing solace to the powerless. It hoped thus to make the rich man in his castle and the poor man at the gate more certain that it was God who had allotted their positions to them.

That Methodism aroused violent opposition is evidence of the deep-seated conservatism of England in the eighteenth century, a sign that only what was familiar and safe was easily tolerated. That Methodism was so successful is evidence of the failure and growing weakness of the old order. Unitarians, Congregationalists, Baptists, Quakers, or — if it could be imagined — Roman Catholics, need only associate themselves with active reform to lose their security. The benevolent squire would become much less easy-going if once he suspected that his leadership was not taken for granted.

In fact, between 1760 and 1789 the peace of English politics was repeatedly broken. Americans, who were tolerated only so long as they were forgotten, dared to assert their independence. John Wilkes experimented in using the mobs of London for a campaign of radicalism instead of for isolated demonstrations of ill-temper. War with France and Spain came almost to invasion. Ireland became harder and harder to manage. India became a financial liability and a scene of passionate disagreements which rolled back to explode in England. Slowly economic development increased the number of problems with which the traditional authorities were not competent to deal. There was already, therefore, a strain upon the old tolerant habits of mind before the French Revolution, with its ideological alarms, aroused all men of respectability to fight for their prejudices.

It was Ireland, and not England, which brought the debate on toleration forward before 1789, and in a practical way. Ireland as a whole, Anglican Ireland as well as dissenting Ireland, had been kept in a subordinate position and treated as inferior to England. It was impossible, in time of war with France and America, to use the full strength of Ireland in England's struggle without making concessions to Irish pride. Of this the Volunteer movement was the visible sign. These guards for the defence of the country (which could free troops for use elsewhere) made demands for their rights as citizens. They would not fight for England unless they were given responsibility and an improved status. It soon appeared that concessions would also have to be made to Roman Catholics as part of the same process of conciliation. Once this argument was admitted for Ireland, its application to England also could be raised.

The problem can be simply stated. Governments must be able to count on the willing co-operation of those they govern. To keep some of their subjects permanently marked by inferiority is prejudicial to the health of the state — or is so once such subjects begin to resent being treated as a special caste. To give every man a stake in society it is not necessary to give him a chance of power, but it is necessary to remove from him the stigma of inferiority. On these arguments Lord Rockingham's friends recommended greater toleration as an answer to the problems of the 1770s and 80s.

Edmund Burke demanded that all men should feel themselves members of the community and co-operate with it whole-heartedly, and that steps should be taken 'to free the government from the weakness and danger of ruling them by force'. But to argue that they were ruled by force so long as penal laws existed was, it was answered, a confession that the old 'natural' hierarchy, with its divisions and spheres of activity, was no longer defensible.

Burke was in a position to feel for all parties in this matter. He had himself a reverence for the past and an affection for the great aristocrats who had dominated the politics of the eighteenth century. He had apprenticed himself to the Whig establishment. He was training his son to profit by his father's achievements so that he might rise even higher in the respectable Anglican world. But Burke himself was the child of an Anglican father and a Roman Catholic mother. He had been born in Ireland and educated in a Quaker school there. All his life he had friends who lived apart from the world of great affairs in sober Quaker peace.

Burke put into words much of the belief held tacitly or even unconsciously in his time about the naturalness of a hierarchical society, a view compared above to that of Aristotle. To most men this conviction seemed reason enough to uphold laws which marked the inferiority of the Irish Roman Catholic, or which allowed English Protestants to control a corporation only under licence. But Burke was so sure of the naturalness of the pattern of society that he wished to let it show itself without artificial aid. He would not have admitted Dissenters into Parliament because that was not the natural place for the sort of men they were. But he would have allowed them to enjoy freely all the civic privileges natural to their position in society. At times he seems to approach the Gladstonian position of seeing positive law as a hindrance to the very purposes such laws were supposed to benefit. As a practical politician, however, he did not always pursue his ideas to their ultimate and inconvenient conclusions. Burke's thought about dissent is in harmony with his views about the colonists; it was not cockets, clearances, or protocol, but affection which should hold the state together.

The movement for relaxation of the laws against dissent was met, as has been said, by an outbreak of that intolerance long concealed behind eighteenth-century habitual attitudes. But there can be little doubt that the forces of aristocratic liberalism would have moved again, and this time more effectively, had the whole situation not been changed by the revolution in France. Prompt upon the heels of the celebration of the centenary of the English revolution came news of the upheaval in Paris. To this news many 'second-class Englishmen' responded with eagerness. Some of the sects famous for radicalism in the seventeenth century had their fire re-kindled. But many of those who had, from positions of authority, been but lately prepared to make concessions to the under-privileged, were startled into antagonism towards those who demanded rights instead of relaxation of the law. Burke, in particular, disliked artificial levelling even more than artificial frontiers between classes of men. He bitterly attacked the Unitarians for propounding egalitarianism. For the rights of man as expounded by Price, Paine, or Parisians, he felt detestation. All his eloquence thereafter was directed against the revolution. He was used, in consequence, as a propagandist for repression and intolerance.

It is not surprising that a theoretical attack upon the bases of society stimulated a more fervent conservatism. When it is remembered that a period of war and of rapid economic change menaced the old order even more insidiously than the doctrines of the radicals, the wonder is that any section of the ruling class remained liberal. But some of Burke's old friends refused to forget the lessons he had formerly expounded. Charles James Fox (once a defender of the full rigidity of Oxford's religious tests) seemed to grow more devoted to the cause of tolerant liberalism in measure as it became unpopular. He fixed upon the Whig party his own attitude to conformity. It became a pose of these Whigs to befriend every under-dog and to defend all losing causes. Above all the emancipation of the Roman Catholics became their most cherished project (particularly as this was an issue which divided their opponents).

For most of the eighteenth century there had been a section of the population which lived peacefully apart and refused respectfully to conform to the standards of the ruling class. By the end of the century there was coming into existence a new and more restless section which, for economic reasons, felt that it did not belong to Old England. A junction of the ideas of these two very different kinds of 'nonconformity' can be seen in the socialist Sunday schools of early nineteenth-century Manchester. They might well have united forces to wage war upon the established order. That they did not was in large measure because part of the aristocracy clung to a faith in liberal toleration. But this faith did not survive unchanged. It was hardened in adversity until it became quite different from that casual inattention which is usually termed toleration earlier in the century: it became a deliberate policy, whereas it had once been a patronising laziness.

'Toleration', says the *Oxford Dictionary of the Christian Church*, 'is generally held to merit commendation when it issues from respect for the natural rights of the human person to freedom of belief, but condemnation when it is due to mere indifference.' For most of the eighteenth century it had been due not exactly to indifference but rather to a confidence of having nothing to meet or to fear, a sense of complete mastery. Yet from the experience of this period some members of the ruling class, men of humane mind, men also of obstinate perversity, evolved those principles for the future which 'merit commendation'.

SUGGESTIONS FOR FURTHER READING

(The most useful books are mentioned first)

Bebb, E. D., *Nonconformity and Social and Economic Life, 1660–1800*, Epworth Press, 1935.

Lincoln, A. H., *Some Political and Social Ideas of English Dissent, 1763–1800*, Cambridge University Press, 1938.

Robbins, Caroline, *The Eighteenth-Century Commonwealthman*, Harvard and Oxford University Press, 1959.

Sykes, N., *Church and State in England in the Eighteenth Century*, Cambridge University Press, 1934.

McLachlan, H., *English Education under the Test Acts; the History of the Nonconformist Academies, 1662–1820*, Manchester.

Ward, B., *The Dawn of the Catholic Revival in England, 1781–1803*, 2 vols., Longmans, 1909.

Edwards, M. L., *John Wesley and the Eighteenth Century; his Social and Political Influence*, Allen & Unwin, 1933.

Jones, M. Gwladys, *The Charity School Movement; Eighteenth-century Puritanism in Action*, Cambridge University Press, 1938.

—— *Hannah More.*

Thomas, R., *Richard Price.*

Palmer, R.R., *The Age of The Democratic Revolution 1760–1800*, vol. 1, *The Challenge*, Princeton, 1959.

II

Party in the Eighteenth Century

by JOHN BROOKE

'Party divisions', wrote Edmund Burke in 1769, 'whether on the whole operating for good or evil, are things inseparable from free government.' It is a remark no sensible person today would disagree with. But the eighteenth century prayed for the extinction of party. 'To unite the hearts of all his Majesty's subjects' was the professed aim even of party leaders. 'Party is the madness of many for the gain of a few', wrote Swift at the beginning of the century; and Wilberforce in 1785 welcomed Pitt's plan of parliamentary reform because it would 'tend to diminish the progress of party'. Few politicians in the eighteenth century would have openly agreed with Burke's dictum.

In the seventeenth century parties took something of their substance from religion. It was an age in which organized religion counted for a good deal, and a party is in politics what a church is in religion. But in the latter half of the century party struggles became more political in character, more concerned to change or to preserve the State rather than the Church. By the time the Hanoverians came to the throne the majority of the political nation was sick to death of party strife. When ecclesiastical squabbling became too much to be borne, Convocation was suppressed; but to suppress Parliament would have been cutting off the nose to spite the face. Hence the dilemma of the eighteenth century. It wanted Parliament, but not party; and it could not see that it must have both or neither.

How was it that the eighteenth century failed to see this very obvious truth? In part the answer lies in the limited purposes for which government existed. Its function was threefold: to conduct foreign policy; to keep law and order; and to maintain conditions in which British commerce could flourish. Parliament's primary role was not to legislate, but to vote supplies and to keep watch on Government; and Government's role was to do as little as possible to interfere with the lives and property of free men, supposed capable of managing their own affairs.

> How small, of all that human hearts endure,
> That part which laws or kings can cause or cure!

Administration, as far as home affairs were concerned, was mainly a matter of following the correct legal precedents; and party divisions arose primarily over the question of who was to be Government, not what Government was to do. There could be little disagreement over policy when Government was not expected to have a policy; and the struggle for power was carried on nakedly and unashamedly, unclothed and unhampered by political ideas. The common eighteenth-century view of politics was that of the Duchess of Omnium, in Trollope's *The Prime Minister*:

> The country goes on its own way, either for better or for worse, whichever of them are in. I don't think it makes any difference as to what sort of laws are passed. But among ourselves, in our set, it makes a deal of difference who gets the garters, and the counties, who are made barons and then earls, and whose name stands at the head of everything.

The question as to who shall rule is basic to every political system; but in politics the struggle for power is dignified as a conflict between opposing political ideas, so much so that historians come to believe that ideas, rather than instinctive aggressive forces, impel men towards conflict. Party divisions are inseparable not merely from free government but from all government; but our moral sense is repelled by man's desire for power unless it is draped in the garment of ideas. Politics in the eighteenth century was at a parting of the ways: it had dropped its concern for religion and not yet developed a concern for economics, and until the 1780s there was no widespread desire for constitutional reform. Party became in effect nothing but a struggle for power: hence its repellent aspect, and the reason why men of high moral principle, mistaking cause for effect, repudiated it.

Yet, ironically, an eighteenth-century Opposition had to have some kind of political programme. It could not play the game of pure politics in an ideological void. Men could not admit, even to themselves, that their aim was simply to get into office, and that once in office their policy would be the same as that of the Government they were opposing. They had to have a programme different from that of the Government; and if there were no grievances amenable to remedy by Parliament, they had to be invented. Otherwise Government and Opposition would be like Tweedledum and Tweedledee, and there would be no reason to prefer the one to the other. The Opposition had to persuade men that the rule of Government was oppressive and would bring the country to ruin, while the rule of Opposition would preserve to them all the blessings of free British subjects, which is exactly what the Opposition has to do today, except that the argument is phrased in economic rather than in constitutional terms. A mass electorate cares more for its material comforts, a restricted electorate for its constitutional rights.

Parliament today is composed entirely of party men, and Opposition cannot normally expect to defeat the Government in the House of Commons. But the electorate is divided into those with a definite party allegiance and the floating voters, who really decide the result of a general election. It is at the polls, not in Parliament, that Opposition hopes to bring down the Government. A good deal of excitement has been taken out of parliamentary proceedings; and by-elections, rather than divisions in the House, have become tests of the Government's standing with public opinion.

In the eighteenth century this situation was reversed. The idea of a general election as a party contest was unknown. The outcome of a general election was the resultant of a number of forces, both local and national. The electorate, though restricted, included many humble and ignorant voters, and lacked genuine political feeling. Nor was there any need to go to all the trouble of fighting an election in the country. In the eighteenth-century House of Commons there was the perfect parallel to the twentieth-century electorate, for the House of Commons contained both party men and independents, or floating voters; and the Government depended for its majority on the independents. If they could be lured away its defeat was certain.

To lure away the independents was no easy task. Most of them disliked party, all cherished their independence. 'A plague on both your houses' was their attitude towards party struggles. Many felt that opposition to the King's Government was factious, or at least that in the argument between the two sides Government should be given the benefit of the doubt. Many were not politicians at all, but valued their seats as family heirlooms, or for the prestige they gave them in their locality. Their attendance was often infrequent, and could never be relied on. The only real chance Opposition had of winning over the independents was when Government lost their confidence through ill success or incompetence in waging war. In short, Opposition could succeed through no efforts of its own, but only through the failure of Government. In quiet times it did not expect to defeat Government, but was satisfied if it could make such a nuisance of itself that Government would think it worth while to buy over its leaders. This was the classic game of Opposition as played by William Pitt, one of its greatest exponents in the first half of the century.

In the words of Professor Butterfield, 'something that we can almost call a stock opposition programme' developed, 'changing little throughout the reigns of the three Georges'. This programme served to give Opposition a respectable façade, to persuade the independents into the belief that the leaders of Opposition were actuated by public principles, not solely by the desire for office. Like most party programmes it started off as a vote-catching device and ended up by being taken seriously — by its inventors as well as by those to whom it was addressed. On one occasion (in 1782), under the stress of a unique national disaster, the programme was actually put into effect when the Opposition achieved power. But usually it was discarded or whittled away to nothing once it had served its purpose.

Probably the best example of an Opposition programme is Edmund Burke's *Thoughts on the Cause of the Present Discontents*, published in 1770. Burke's charge against the Administration of Lord North (stripped down to its essentials) is that of Pulteney against Walpole or of Charles James Fox against the younger Pitt. The constitution was in danger through the excessive influence of the Crown. Government, through its control of patronage, had corrupted a majority of the House of Commons, and Parliament was no longer representative of the nation. The remedy was to restore the freedom of Parliament by reducing the influence of the Crown. But, since fashions change, Burke's proposals were somewhat different from those in vogue in the earlier part of the century, though their effect was intended to be the same. Instead of disabling junior officers of the Army and Navy from sitting in Parliament, Burke proposed to disable contractors; instead of a Place Bill, he advocated the reduction of sinecures; instead of shorter Parliaments, the disfranchisement of revenue officers. Here is the 'stock opposition programme' of which Professor Butterfield writes. Whig 'economical reform' is but the old Tory programme writ large.

This programme is not to be identified with any political group or tradition. It was neither a Whig nor a Tory programme, it was an Opposition programme. In the late seventeenth century it was the Whigs who tried to reduce the influence of the Crown — in Charles II's reign they even tried to change the succession. Under the first two Georges, when the Ministers were Whigs, it became a Tory programme. Under George III the Rockingham party, the Opposition of those days, adopted the policy of the Tories and called themselves the heirs of the Whigs. Government, on the other hand, whether Whig or Tory, always sought to preserve undiminished the influence of the Crown. In the Regency crisis of 1788 the younger Pitt, aware that he could not expect to remain in office if the Prince of Wales became Regent, sought to cut down the powers of the Regency. His opponent, Charles James Fox, who a few years before had been all for reducing the authority of the Crown, now that he saw himself on the threshold of office contended for full powers for the Regent. 'Surely Mr. Fox will not call his doctrine a Whig one?',

B

asked one bewildered M.P., forgetting that under Walpole and the Pelhams the Whigs had always upheld the influence of the Crown.

How do Whigs and Tories fit into this picture? There were Whigs and Tories in the seventeenth century and in the eighteenth too, yet the names cannot be equated or put forward as evidence of a continuous tradition. 'While ideas outlive reality', wrote Sir Lewis Namier, 'names and words outlast both.' The Whig and Tory tradition was most active in the sphere of religion, where it lasted so long as organized religion remained a force in British politics.

In any system of representative government the Crown must take a stand against the growth of party, which, by limiting the Crown's choice of Ministers, restricts its power. Only in an established constitutional monarchy can the Crown become openly dissociated from party. In the eighteenth century the King as head of the executive had the formal right to choose his Ministers for himself: there was no party system to make the choice for him. But he was limited by the necessity to choose Ministers who were acceptable to Parliament. Neither Crown nor Parliament could force a Minister upon the other.

In practice it was impossible to demarcate the boundary between the authority of the Crown and that of Parliament. But time worked against the Crown; and while the power of Parliament imperceptibly increased, that of the Crown diminished. Though the theory of the British constitution requires that the King never dies, the demise of the Crown was always followed by a diminution of its authority. Since the Revolution each monarch has handed on to his successor less authority than he received from his predecessor.

Lord Waldegrave, writing shortly before the accession

of George III, described the political situation in the first half of the century:

> When the Hanover succession took place, the Whigs became the possessors of all the great offices and other lucrative employments; since which time, instead of quarrelling with the prerogative, they have been the champions of every Administration.
>
> However, they have not always been united in one body, under one general, like a regular and well-disciplined army: but may be more aptly compared to an alliance of different clans, fighting in the same cause, professing the same principles, but influenced and guided by their different chieftains.

The first two Georges naturally required a firm adherence to the Hanoverian succession as a qualification for office; and the Tories, Jacobites, or suspected Jacobites, were proscribed, and in time ceased to exist as a party. Some accepted the Hanoverian succession as a *fait accompli* which could not be undone without causing more mischief than it was worth: they acknowledged the Hanoverian King but would not serve him. Others, in varying degrees, remained Jacobites. But since Jacobitism could not openly be advocated without risk to life or estate, it never became a parliamentary programme. It was an underground movement, looking to France for support, and after the failure of the '45 it ceased to exist as a serious political force. Burke in 1751 described the Jacobites as 'a sort of people whose politics consist in wishing that right may take place, and their religion in heartily hating Presbyterians.'

The Whigs thus monopolized Government; and, as Waldegrave says, became champions of the prerogative which now worked in their favour. Divided into their separate clans, they struggled against each other for office; and those who were out naturally tended to form an alliance with the Tories and with the independent members who opposed Administration.

To complete the picture of politics under the first two Georges, there is the party of the Prince of Wales. It needs no political reason to explain why the Hanoverian Kings always quarrelled with their heirs apparent: the conflict between one generation and the next is as much a part of human life as birth itself. In a constitutional monarchy this conflict would have had little political effect; in the eighteenth century it led to the formation of a Prince's party. The Prince had an amount of patronage to dispense second only to that of the King, and to present favours were added hopes of even greater benefits in the future. Not every politician in Opposition joined the Prince, nor did he ever become the leader of the Opposition. He was merely one of a group of contending party leaders. Naturally he adopted the stock Opposition programme, and advocated measures to reduce the influence of the Crown he would one day inherit.

George II, as Prince of Wales, intended when he came to the throne to dismiss his father's Minister, Sir Robert Walpole, and appoint his own. But in 1727 the incompetence of Spencer Compton, his intended Minister, forced him to retain Walpole, who remained for another fifteen years. George III, as Prince of Wales, also intended when he came to the throne to dismiss his predecessor's Ministers and appoint his own, and unlike George II carried out his intention. Thus the accession of George III brought a change in the political scene which the accession of George II had not done. Also, by 1760 Jacobitism was dead; and the accession of a new King, 'born and bred in this country' and without his predecessor's German predilections, was taken by many Tories as the occasion to make their peace with the Hanoverian dynasty. The accession of George III saw the end of the Tories as a recognizable group in Parliament. The name continued to be used, but only by Opposition Whigs as a term of abuse for their opponents. Its use for the party which grew up after 1784 under the younger Pitt belongs to the nineteenth century.

Lord Holland, grandson of Henry Fox and nephew of Charles James, wrote in his *Memoirs of the Whig Party*:

> The truth is that the parliamentary cabals which divided the Court during the reign of George II and the first twelve years of George III, being mere struggles for favour and power, created more real blood and personal rancour between individuals than the great questions of policy and principle which arose on the American and French wars.

By the time Lord North assumed office in 1770 most of the Opposition Whigs were grouped under the leadership of Lord Rockingham, with Edmund Burke as his fugleman. The Rockingham Whigs claimed descent from the party of Newcastle, Henry Pelham, and Sir Robert Walpole, a claim which cannot be substantiated either in respect of personnel or political ideas. Rockingham himself had been a friend and political ally of Newcastle, but the majority of his followers had had no connection with the Pelhams, and a substantial number came of Tory families (Dowdeswell, Rockingham's most trusted adviser and until his death in 1775 leader of the party in the Commons, was a former Tory). As for political ideas, the Rockinghams simply adopted the stock Opposition programme, but gave it a new twist. Once again the undue influence of the Crown was held to be 'the cause of the present discontents'; and Burke explained the short-lived ministries of George III's reign as a deliberate attempt, 'conceived by some persons in the Court of Frederick, Prince of Wales', to 'secure to the Court the unlimited and uncontrolled use of its own vast influence'. Burke's apologia for the Rockingham party is the most elaborate (and far-fetched) of the century, but really it all boils down to this: that no drastic changes were needed in the constitution, and things would go right again if only George III would make Rockingham his Minister.

Burke's defence of party was uncorrelated to the realities of eighteenth-century politics:

How men can proceed without any connexion at all is to me utterly incomprehensible. Of what sort of materials must that man be made . . . who can sit whole years in Parliament with five hundred and fifty of his fellow citizens . . . without seeing any one sort of men whose character, conduct, or disposition would lead him to associate himself with them, to aid and be aided, in any one system of public utility?

Yet the highest virtue to which an eighteenth-century M.P. could lay claim was independence — both of party and the Crown. The majority of the House, not obliged either to the Crown or to a patron for their seats, could claim to be independent; and only at times of national crisis or when a real political principle was at stake could they be induced to act in party. Even so, they rarely surrendered their independence, and few were wholly reliable.

Burke never claimed that the Cabinet should be formed from one party only. The Rockingham group at its largest was never more than about a fifth of the House. Burke demanded what he called a 'united Administration', which implied

the necessity of having the great strongholds of government in well-united hands, in order to secure the predominance of right and uniform principles; of having the capital offices of deliberation and execution of those who can deliberate with mutual confidence, and who will execute what is resolved with firmness and fidelity.

An admirable principle; but the Rockinghams could not put it into effect when they came into office in 1782. In that Cabinet Rockingham's followers were in a minority: on the crucial issue of the recognition of American independence they were out-voted; and the responsibility for negotiating peace with America was in the hands of Shelburne, whom the Rockinghams regarded as little better than an enemy. In short, when the Rockinghams came to power Burke's ideas on party government were found to be unworkable.

It needed a 'great question of policy and principle' to rouse the independents and extend the radius of party beyond the professional politician. On the American war a considerable, but amorphous, Opposition ranged itself against the Government, of which the Rockingham group formed the nucleus. Yet the American war was not an issue on which parties could take up a lasting alignment. Both Government and Opposition held that Britain was sovereign over the colonies. Their differences were concerned over the degree to which sovereignty should be exercised, and particularly as to whether the Americans were justified or not in their rebellion. The war would end one day, and these issues would be settled; while it continued, it was the source of genuine, but not lasting, party divisions. In fact the Opposition fell to pieces once the war was over.

The American war showed the weakness of Burke's conception of party. 'The great and only foundation of government', he wrote in the *Present Discontents*, was 'the confidence of the people.' But during the period of the American war the confidence of the people was plainly given to Lord North, not to Rockingham.

The generality of the people of England (Rockingham wrote to Burke on Sept. 24, 1775) are now led away by the mis-

> representations and arts of the Ministry . . . so that the
> violent measures towards America are fairly adopted and
> countenanced by a majority of individuals of all ranks,
> professions, or occupations in this country . . . and I con-
> ceive that nothing but a degree of experience of the evils can
> bring about a right judgment in the public at large.

And Burke to Rockingham on Oct. 26, 1777: 'We can do
nothing essential unless the great change of sentiments
arise in the *public*.' The Rockinghams could only stand
helplessly by and wait for British defeats to bring over
opinion to their side. They had no roots in the nation at
large, no broad basis of support from which to lead a campaign against the war. They were a knot of discontented
politicians, not the leaders of a nation-wide party. Burke,
an Irishman and profoundly ignorant of the nature of
English social life, believed that the magnates of the
Rockingham party should use their position in their counties and rouse the freeholders, gentry, and merchants into
a campaign of protest against the war. But Rockingham
knew better: he could only follow and try to direct opinion,
he could not drive it; and he would not risk his position in
his county by attempting to do so. 'I would not give any
handle in Yorkshire for Yorkshiremen to say that my
politics had led them beyond their intentions, or that I
had checked their well-founded ardour', he wrote about
the petitioning movement of 1769; and his attitude was
the same during the American war. Burke, disillusioned at
his failure to stir his party leaders into action, wrote about
them to Fox on Oct. 8, 1777: 'A great deal of activity
and enterprise can scarcely ever be expected from such
men, unless some horrible calamity is just over their heads
or unless they suffer some gross personal insults from
power.'

The Government's failure to subdue America, the intervention of France and Spain, and the subsequent danger of invasion, were the conditions under which a new Radical movement arose. Radicalism had previously existed in London and a few large towns, but had never attracted the squirearchy. The movement of 1779 began in Yorkshire, was supported mainly by the smaller gentry and freeholders, and was independent of the parliamentary Opposition. It was aimed primarily not against the war, but at what it regarded as excessive Government expenditure on places, pensions, and sinecures — against the excessive influence of the Crown. So far the Rockinghams approved, but the Association movement went far beyond the Rockinghams in demanding parliamentary reform as the cure. Rockingham was frightened at the growth of a movement he could not control, which threatened to usurp the lead in Yorkshire politics, and to introduce unwelcome changes into the constitution. He set his face against all 'speculative changes', and tried to rally his supporters behind a moderate programme of reform: Burke's Economical Reform Bill, which reformed the Royal Household, and abolished a number of sinecures tenable with a seat in Parliament; Jennings Clerke's bill disabling Government contractors from sitting in the House; and Crewe's bill disfranchising revenue officers.

The House of Commons voted on 6 April, 1780, that 'the influence of the Crown has increased, is increasing, and ought to be diminished' — a resolution which embodied the stock Opposition programme of the century. But Parliament refused to advance beyond this general grievance, and North's Administration was strong enough to prevent any part of the Opposition's programme from becoming law. While the Government was being pressed hard on economical reform, it had a comfortable majority on American questions. And it was only after Cornwallis's surrender at Yorktown that the House of Commons lost confidence in North's conduct of the war.

The King could not retain North after he had lost the confidence of the Commons, nor could the Commons force the King to keep Fox as Minister. By 1783 party organization in Parliament was much more rigid than it had been at the beginning of the American war; the practice of Government and Opposition benches had taken root; the younger Pitt approximated to the position of a modern Prime Minister and Charles Fox to a modern Leader of the Opposition. The general election of 1784 was something like an appeal to the country, and public opinion played a larger part than it had ever done. Yet it was not party but the Crown which had placed Pitt in office.

The Whig Opposition had reduced the influence of the Crown over Parliament, yet in 1784 the Crown was able to secure a Parliament which would support the Minister of its choice. According to Burke, the reforms of 1782–3 had gone far enough, and to go any further would be an unwarrantable infringement on the constitution. But there were many Members who believed that Parliament would never be sufficiently responsive to public opinion until the constituencies had been reformed. Parliamentary reform was not a party issue. Pitt introduced it, and Fox supported it, yet it was rejected by the House of Commons.

The Liberal and Conservative parties which governed Britain in the nineteenth century have their origin in the period of the French Revolution. The ideas of the French Revolution had long been present in Britain below the surface of parliamentary politics: events in France brought them into Parliament, and led to new party alignments. Fox rejoiced at the news of the fall of the Bastille, and, though he deplored the bloody progress of the Revolution, opposed the attempts of the European powers to put it down. It was Edmund Burke, a fellow Whig, who inspired the policy of intervention against the Revolution. 'You seem in everything to have strayed out of the high road of nature', he wrote in his *Reflections on the French Revolution*. 'The property of France does not govern it.' And he defined Jacobinism as 'the revolt of the enterprising talents of a country against its property'. The Revolution did not make Burke a Conservative, as Macaulay believed: he had been one all along, but there had been no occasion on which he had to declare himself. Under his influence a substantial part of the Whigs deserted Fox and took office under Pitt. Portland, who had succeeded Rockingham as titular leader of the party, became Home Secretary, charged with the suppression of revolutionary principles in Britain at the expense of freedom of speech and writing. The Conservative party of today springs from the union of Pitt and the Portland Whigs in 1794: beyond that its genealogy is spurious.

In this respect Burke may be said to be the prophet of Conservatism. But one of the strongest assets of the British Conservative party has been its ability to accept, and profit from, radical changes introduced against its will. Under Peel it accepted the reformed Parliament; under Disraeli free trade; under its present leaders the welfare state. British Conservatism tries to slow down the clock, not to set it back. None of this flexibility is derived from Burke. Burke's Conservatism was based on the divine right of property to govern. On this principle, he believed, depended the survival of morality and Christianity; and there could be no compromise with Jacobinism. Burke saw with horror the holy war he had preached against the French regicides turn into the familiar scramble for colonies. He wanted a war not against France but against Jacobinism; and the capture of a West Indian island did nothing to forward the restoration of the Bourbons, or of the French Church to its old privileged position. Burke was the prophet not of British Conservatism but of European reaction; and his true disciples were Gentz and Metternich, not Peel and Disraeli.

The old cry of the undue influence of the Crown begins to drop out of party discourses about the time of the French Revolution. Two parties begin to take issue on lines familiar in the nineteenth century: one emphasizing authority and order, the other liberty and reform.

Towards the end of the eighteenth century the range and complexity of government was increasing enormously. The Napoleonic wars and the growth of Britain into an industrial power forced Government to pay continuous attention to problems with which it had hitherto been only occasionally concerned, and to some which no one had thought the concern of Government. Parliament became increasingly occupied with legislation of a controversial nature, which stimulated party divisions. As government became more complex the Cabinet strengthened its authority against the King. He could still block measures, as he did Catholic emancipation; but could no longer personally superintend the working of the government machine. The centre of power shifted from the King's Closet to the Cabinet room. The growth of parties limited his choice of Ministers, and a wider informed public opinion began to make itself felt in politics. For a long time two conceptions — the King as active head of the executive and the King as constitutional monarch — existed side by side; but one was of the past and the other of the future.

The story of the growth of party government lies outside the eighteenth century, and has yet to be told in detail.

SUGGESTIONS FOR FURTHER READING

Feiling, K., *The Second Tory Party, 1714–1832,* Macmillan, 1938.

Butterfield, H., *George III, Lord North and the People*, G. Bell, 1949.

Namier, L., *Personalities and Powers*, Hamish Hamilton, 1955. The Romanes lecture: *Monarchy and the Party System* is reprinted in this book.

Brooke, J., *The Chatham Administration, 1766–1768*, Macmillan, 1956.

Owen, J. B., *The Rise of the Pelhams*, Methuen, 1957.

Christie, I. R., *The End of North's Administration*, Macmillan, 1958.

———

Burke, E., *The Works of the Right Honourable Edmund Burke*, Oxford University Press (World's Classics), 1906.
Observations on a late 'State of the Nation' (last few pages).
Thoughts on the Cause of the Present Discontents.
Reflections on the French Revolution.
An Appeal from the New to the Old Whigs.
Letters on a Regicide Peace (last two letters).

Frederick, Prince of Wales

by BETTY KEMP

FREDERICK Louis, eldest child of George Augustus, Electoral Prince of Hanover, and his wife Caroline of Ansbach, was born on Jan. 6, 1707, in the palace of Herrenhausen. He remained in Hanover when his grandfather became George I of Great Britain in 1714, and again when his father became George II in 1727. George I created him Duke of Gloucester in 1717, Knight of the Garter in 1718 and Duke of Edinburgh in 1727. In December, 1728, in response to Walpole's insistence, Frederick was brought to England. He never left it again. In January, 1729, he was created Prince of Wales. He was given no public function in England and had no part in the administration of the country during any of his father's visits to Hanover. In April, 1736, Frederick married Augusta, daughter of the Duke of Saxe-Gotha. George II then granted him, from the Civil List, an income of £50,000 — half the sum he had himself received as Prince of Wales. With the revenues from the Duchy of Cornwall, Frederick's income was rather less than £60,000 a year. This was certainly inadequate. In July, 1737, Frederick's first child, Augusta, was born, and in September he was expelled from the Court of St. James. Thereafter, though his official residence was Leicester House, he lived mainly at Carlton House and at his country houses — Kew House, or the White House, and Cliveden in Buckinghamshire. In 1742 his income

from the Civil List was increased to £100,000 and he and
his father were superficially reconciled. He had six more
children: George, the future George III, was born in 1738,
Edward in 1739, William Henry in 1743, Henry Frederick
in 1745, Frederick William in 1750 and Caroline Matilda
in 1751.

An heir to the throne who dies before he reaches it can
hardly escape a distorted reputation, especially if there has
been antagonism between him and the reigning King.
Perhaps this antagonism is, in Stubbs's phrase, 'the inevitable bane of royalty', but in the normal course of
events the heir who inflicts it is judged not by that but by
his later kingship. A good king's reputation, indeed, may
be enhanced if he has been an irresponsible or factious
heir, for then the assumption of the Crown is seen to be
ennobling. So it was, in the fifteenth century, with Henry
V of England, a King much admired by Frederick. The
reputation of an heir who never becomes King may, on
the other hand, be enhanced if he has had some chance to
prove his capacity for affairs. The last Prince of Wales to
die before coming to the throne was Henry, eldest son of
James I, and accused by him of wishing 'to bury me alive'.
He sat on the Council and was concerned in the management of the navy before he died in 1612 at the age of
eighteen; Frederick, in his twenty-three years in England,
had no political duty of any kind.

There are other reasons why Frederick's reputation has
been distorted. The best-known chroniclers of George II's
reign — Hervey and Horace Walpole — both hated him.
They agreed in their determination to show that his quarrels with his father, far from being inevitable, were the
consequence of his character: vicious, vain, incompetent
and unreliable. 'He was indeed', wrote Hervey, 'as false as
his capacity would allow him to be, and was more capable

in that walk than in any other.' Hervey's hatred of Frederick, as contemporaries knew, was the result of failure to control him, and, in revenge, he vilified Frederick to the King and Queen; Horace Walpole's hatred of Frederick was the result of his share in bringing about the fall of Sir Robert Walpole in 1742. Horace Walpole's *Memoirs of the Reign of George II* were first published in 1822, Hervey's *Memoirs of the Reign of George II* in 1848. Although both men are known to be quite unscrupulous where their personal feelings are aroused, Frederick's reputation still rests almost entirely on their testimony. This is of course very largely concerned with the hostility between Frederick and his father. Here, even without their testimony, Frederick's reputation would perhaps have suffered by reason of the fact that this hostility was, in part, played out in politics, and, like all hostility between the Hanoverians and their heirs, has come to be regarded merely as a normal feature of the eighteenth-century political scene.

Pitt once spoke of 'exploding Horace Walpole'. A step towards this can be taken, perhaps, by indicating some of those things which accounted for Frederick's popularity in the country — a popularity not denied by Hervey and Horace Walpole, but explained by them as an affectation, assumed to spite the King. Frederick was gay, generous, impulsive; he had easy and informal manners. He enjoyed meeting people of all classes. In 1735 he expressed 'a great inclination to make a progress'; this, thought Lady Irwin, 'will never be allowed till he is King, his popularity having already given great offence; so nothing will be suffered to increase that.'

Frederick's patronage of men of letters contrasted with — perhaps compensated for — the lack of it in his father and grandfather. Swift in 1739 wrote of the 'Golden Age' when he should be King and 'restorer of the Libertyes of his People'. Pope presented him with a set of his works and with the dog which regularly accompanied him on his walks at Kew; he gave Pope busts of philosophers for his library and urns for his garden. James Thomson dedicated his poem 'Liberty' to Frederick. Lesser poets — James Hammond, Richard Glover, Richard West — frequented his Court, David Mallett became his Under-Secretary, George Lyttelton his Secretary. Paul Whitehead, 'a notorious but not inconsiderable poet', sang his praises. George Dodington, patron of poets and lifelong friend of Voltaire, sent to his friends in Italy for ornaments for Frederick's gardens. And, in 1742, James Oswald sought to promote the success of David Hume's *Essays, Moral and Political*, by planning to 'excite the Curiosity' of members of Frederick's Court who, he wrote, 'seem to have a very good Taste'.

Two of the leading scientists of the day were amongst Frederick's friends. John Theophilus Desaguliers, son of a Huguenot refugee, physicist and astronomer, inventor of the planetarium, was a member of Frederick's household. In 1737 Desaguliers set up his planetarium at one end of a large room at the top of Frederick's house at Kew, with 'all his mathematical and mechanical instruments' at the other end. There he read his lectures 'every day, which the Prince diligently attends'. Desaguliers was a renowned lecturer, and published his lectures in 1738. He was a Freemason, and in 1737, in a ceremony held at Kew, admitted Frederick as a Master Mason. Stephen Hales, botanist and plant physiologist, inventor of the ventilator and founder of the Society of Arts, was often visited by Frederick at Teddington, where Hales was perpetual curate. Frederick's zeal for botany infected his family — Samuel Lysons remarked in 1792, in his *History of Surrey*, that 'the present royal family is greatly attached to the study of botany' — and was one of the interests he shared with Bute, whose friendship with him began in 1747. Frederick's collection of exotic plants and trees at Kew, which he planned to make into a centre of botanical research, was extended after his death by Princess Augusta, with the assistance of Bute and Prince George. It formed the basis of the Physic or Exotic Garden which was founded in 1759 and in 1840 became the Royal Botanic Gardens.

In another branch of gardening Frederick was also a pioneer: he led the way in the change of taste from the formal gardens of the early eighteenth century to the natural, landscaped gardens of the second half of the century, usually associated with Capability Brown. In this his assistant was the versatile William Kent, whose pupil Brown was, and the scene of his activities was the ten or so acres of garden at Carlton House. The house was acquired for Frederick by Lord Chesterfield in 1732; it was then described by James Ralph as 'delightfully situated . . . hardly any place is capable of greater improvements, and hardly any place stands in more need of them.' By 1734 Frederick's improvements, according to Sir Thomas Robinson, had made 'the Prince's garden ... more diversified and of greater variety than anything of that compass I ever saw . . . it has the appearance of beautiful nature, and without being told, one would imagine art had no part in the finishing.' Frederick's success created 'a new taste in gardening', and even by the end of 1734 Robinson noted that 'the celebrated gardens of Claremont, Chiswick and Stowe are full of labourers, to modernize the expensive works finished in them, even since everyone's memory.' Frederick's gardens at Kew House were already famed for their beauty when Frederick acquired the house, about 1730, on a long lease from the Capel family. They were a constant source of delight to him from then until his death, and he never tired of replanning them and of working in them himself. His Court, Dodington remarks, were also made to work there. George Vertue, antiquary and engraver, visited Kew in 1750 and described Frederick's 'contrivances, designs of his improvements in his gardens, water works, canal &c; — great number of people labouring there; his new Chinese summer-house; painted in their state and ornaments the story of Confucius and his doctrines.'

Frederick's discriminating taste and his love and knowledge of pictures is attested by Vertue, whom he employed to make catalogues both of the royal collections and of his own collections. His 'affection and inclination to promote and encourage Art and Artists', Vertue wrote in 1749, 'is daily more and more evident, from the employments he has given several Artists, and by his delights in conversations and his purchases of paintings and pictures, Miniatures, enamells etc.' In 1749, too, Frederick discussed with Vertue a plan for an 'Academy for drawing and painting' under royal patronage; this might, if he had lived, have anticipated the Royal Academy, founded in 1768. He was interested in antiquities and had contacts both with the Society of Dilettanti — to which several members of his Household belonged — and with the Society of Antiquaries, which just before his death was hoping for his assistance in obtaining a Charter.

Frederick's recreations were certainly such as endear a prince to his people. Horse-racing, patronized by royalty all through the seventeenth century and until 1714, but dropped by George I and George II, was taken up again by Frederick. He loved sailing on the Thames, and employed Kent to build for him the beautiful Chinese barge — 'not Cleopatra's upon the river Cydnus was more elegant', thought Lady Irwin — which was used as a royal barge until 1849 and is now in the National Maritime Museum at Greenwich. From this barge, on Prince George's eleventh birthday in 1749, Frederick watched a race of oarsmen from Whitehall to Putney, and presented the winner with a silver cup; in the same year he organized and took part in a race of yachts and pleasure-boats to the Nore and back. He played cricket, watched cricket matches, and was the first patron of the Surrey County Cricket team. He was an enthusiastic producer of plays, especially at Cliveden, and in this was helped by Quin, who taught 'the boy [Prince George] to speak'. He arranged concerts, often at one of his houses, and himself played on the cello. At Kew he lived 'quite in private, without form', walking, gardening, and planning river picnics.

In all these activities there appear the 'great affability' and 'easy familiarity' which pleased Lady Irwin in 1735. Vertue, after Frederick's death, praised the same qualities. With all his 'heroic virtues', he wrote, this 'great and good prince' was 'conversable and void of ceremony and pride as any man living'.

There can be no doubt that Frederick's quarrel with his father had political significance. The antagonism between them is, indeed, usually taken as the archetype of the antagonism between all the Hanoverians and their heirs. The form this antagonism took, it is said, was determined by the nature of the Hanoverian monarchy. This is true. It was a mixed, constitutional monarchy, characterized above all by the fact that, although the king's prerogative of choosing his ministers was not challenged in theory, it was challenged — or at least hampered — in practice by the increasing ability of the House of Commons to obtain the resignation or even the dismissal of ministers it disliked. The king and his ministers were therefore faced with a series of opposition groups in Parliament, struggling not only to make opposition effective — by forcing a change of ministers — but also to win for opposition an accepted place in constitutional theory. An opposition enrolled under the banner of a Prince of Wales, the heir to the throne, it is argued, seemed more 'constitutional' than one which did not have his support, and an opposition which gained his leadership, or at least his approval, achieved thereby a colour of respectability.

This is a generalized picture, and, when applied to Frederick's relations with his father, and to his political activities, is seen to require some modification. George II's own quarrel with his father in 1717, when Prince of Wales, certainly helps to explain why, from the beginning, he was suspicious of Frederick, as it helps to explain why Walpole tried to prevent a breach between them. But other factors, not primarily connected with English domestic politics, contributed to George II's dislike of his heir. One was the question of Frederick's marriage. In 1723, as a corollary of the Treaty of Charlottenburg between England and Prussia, it was suggested that Frederick should marry his cousin Wilhelmina, daughter of Frederick William I of Prussia, and that her brother Frederick (later Frederick the Great) should marry Frederick's sister Amelia. The treaty was part of Townshend's scheme for a network of alliances against the Emperor. The scheme itself was short-lived, and the 'double marriage project' was perhaps doomed from the start. Neither George I nor Frederick William really welcomed it, because of the traditional hostility of Hanover and Prussia, and it hung fire mainly, perhaps, because of Prussia's growing inclination to seek an alliance with the Emperor instead of with his enemies. She made one, secretly, in October, 1726. The accession of George II, who much disliked and was disliked by his brother-in-law Frederick William, was a further obstacle. In 1728 Prussia concluded a formal alliance with the Emperor and relations between England and Prussia rapidly worsened. Nevertheless, in 1728 Frederick rashly tried to promote his own marriage. His attempt led to bitter dissensions in the Prussian royal family and provoked the anger of George II. After the fall of Townshend in 1730 his anti-Imperial policy lapsed, and in May, 1731, Walpole made the Treaty of Vienna with the Emperor. Walpole was not, however, averse from the marriage alliance with Prussia, and Frederick remained openly anxious for it. The last attempt to secure it, in 1730, failed simply for personal reasons: a sudden outburst of anger against George II caused Frederick William to break off negotiations and make arrangements to marry his son and daughter within Germany. Although George II had not wanted the marriages, he never forgave Frederick William for this insult, and Frederick's readiness for the alliance seemed only a further affront.

Relations between Frederick and George II were also affected by the question of dissolving the personal union between England and Hanover. In England, in the first half of the eighteenth century, there was frequent complaint that, as William Murray said in 1744, 'Hanover is a millstone about our necks, and . . . neither would nor could be borne with.' Nevertheless, the idea of dissolving the union was, in the beginning, conceived in the interests rather of Hanover than of England. Soon after George I's accession he suggested to his English ministers that he might make provision in his will for the separation of the two countries after his death. Although they informed him that, in their opinion, it was not possible thus to set aside the Act of Settlement, he did in fact make a will providing that, after his death, Hanover should be ruled not by his son but by his cousin, the Duke of Brunswick-Wolfenbüttel. George II, being informed by both his English and his Hanoverian ministers that the will was 'illegal and invalid', destroyed it. George II himself was attracted by the idea of separation, but his plan for it was different from his father's. In 1725, before he became King, he expressed the wish that on his death Hanover should be ruled by Frederick, and England by his younger son William, born in England in 1721. Clearly, this plan was more likely to be realized if Frederick remained in Hanover during his father's reign, and perhaps George intended this to happen. He brought Frederick to England in 1728 unwillingly, and only because Walpole convinced him that the matter of Frederick's absence, if further prolonged, would be raised in Parliament. Although the question of dissolving the personal union was raised again later in George II's reign, it was never again suggested that Frederick should not rule England. In 1737 it was rumoured that Frederick would raise the question himself, proposing that, on George II's death, William should become Elector of Hanover. In 1741, on the eve of Walpole's fall, George asked Walpole whether Parliament would be likely to approve this arrangement. Walpole thought that it would. No steps were taken to discover Parliament's opinion, however, partly because the time was inopportune and partly because the Emperor was expected to refuse his consent. Separation was discussed in 1744, when the parliamentary opposition was convinced that Carteret's foreign policy was Hanoverian, not English, in its aims, and George II, in face of Carteret's unpopularity, again suggested raising the matter himself. But nothing was done. Frederick himself, it seems, grew more and more convinced of the 'wiseness of this project' conceived by his grandfather, and clearly believed that his father would do nothing about it. In January

1749, Frederick drew up a set of 'Instructions for my son George', advocating separation as a means of extinguishing 'the jealousies . . . in this Kingdom against the Electorate'. He recommended it also as a means of killing Jacobitism which, by its repercussions on the policy of the European powers, had certainly harmed Hanover. Accordingly he urged George, when he should be King, to promote an Act of Parliament establishing that, after him, no member of his House should rule both England and Hanover.

The contribution of Frederick's political activities to constitutional theory is difficult to assess, but it seems to be smaller than the general picture of opposition between the Hanoverians and their heirs might suggest. 'Formed opposition' was certainly deprecated in the eighteenth century, on the grounds that it challenged the king's prerogative of choosing his ministers. Nevertheless, a series of oppositions existed. They usually claimed, with some justice, that they were not 'formed', but were the expression of occasional dissatisfaction with the policy of the king's ministers, and they were, from time to time, successful in bringing about a change of ministers. Their success, however, in George II's reign, did not always, nor certainly, depend on Frederick's support: they succeeded without his support in 1744, failed with it in 1737 and 1747, and even in 1742 would perhaps have succeeded without it. Moreover, the theory most frequently used to justify opposition — that the king must be saved from evil counsellors — was used irrespective of the presence of the heir in the opposition. It was used in 1741 against Walpole, and in 1744 and 1746 against Carteret, as it was used later, in 1763, against Bute. To George II and his ministers, Frederick's support of opposition did not make opposition more acceptable, though it might make it more dangerous. To many of their contemporaries, too, his support of opposition was primarily a sign of a 'further unhappy breach between a father and his son', tending, as Dodington said in 1737 when he tried to prevent the discussion of Frederick's income in Parliament, to weaken a royal family 'which we have, at last, happily placed upon the Throne'.

To the opposition, on the other hand, there could be no doubt of the usefulness of Frederick's support. For he could save the opposition from the charge of Jacobitism and, by doing so, enable discontented Whigs to strengthen themselves by an alliance with Tories. This was clearly understood by Wyndham, who led the Tories until his death in 1740, and above all by Bolingbroke, who, whether in or out of England, continually urged the wisdom of persuading Frederick to act as the figure-head of a united opposition, a 'national party'. Moreover, an opposition of this kind could hope to act as a focus for discontent which might otherwise have become disaffection: the Jacobite Carte in 1743 comforted the Pretender by reporting to him that, as Frederick was not then opposing the Government, people 'in case of discontent will naturally look for redress from another quarter.' This being so, then an opposition linked with Frederick could hope to attract to itself those moderate Jacobites who, by the 1730s, were concerned rather with condemning particular aspects of Hanoverian government — placemen, long parliaments, corruption, for example — than with seriously plotting to restore the Stuarts. This kind of Jacobitism certainly existed: Frederick openly appealed to it after 1746, and Horace Walpole labelled him a Jacobite. If the 'bane of royalty' was — as Macaulay claimed — not a weakness but a strength to the monarchy in George II's reign, this was because it weakened Jacobitism by providing an alternative way of opposing certain facets of the Hanoverian political system.

Nevertheless, Frederick's political opposition was intermittent. It was first openly expressed in Parliament in the mid-1730s, in the period of disillusionment which followed the opposition's failure to dislodge Walpole after the Excise Bill crisis in 1733 and their failure to embarrass him in 1734 by their attempts to repeal the Test Act and the Septennial Act. In 1737 Frederick accepted a plan (mooted in 1735, and thought to be Bolingbroke's) to raise the question of his income in Parliament, with a view to persuading Parliament to ask the King to increase the amount he allowed Frederick from the Civil List. His supporters in Parliament were, in the main, discontented Whigs, especially Carteret and Pulteney, who took the initiative, and the Cobham group, who had been in opposition since the Excise Bill and in close touch with Frederick since 1735. Nearly half of the Tories (including Wyndham), whose support was essential to victory, abstained. Even so, the majority for the Government in the House of Commons was only thirty. After this, Frederick's opposition came in two main periods: in 1741–2, when it formed part of the general opposition which in March, 1742, at last caused Walpole to resign; and in 1747–51, when it failed in its aim of removing Pelham. Between these periods, from 1742 to 1747, Frederick was, on the whole, a supporter of Government. Although he was at first disappointed with the composition of the Government which succeeded Walpole's, he soon supported it enthusiastically for the sake of Carteret, of whose foreign policy, by 1744, Frederick and George II were almost the only defenders; after November, 1744, he was willing, at first, to acquiesce in Pelham's Broadbottom administration, although it excluded Carteret, because he approved the principle on which it was based. After February, 1746, when Carteret (now Earl Granville) failed to form a

Government, Frederick's acquiescence came to an end, and by the end of the year he was in opposition again.

In none of these phases is it possible to contend that Frederick's participation in politics was decisive: it was most effective in 1741–2, and least so in 1744, when he tried to strengthen Carteret against the increasing hostility of his colleagues and of Parliament. Nevertheless, for the whole of the period from 1737 to 1751, Frederick was a force to be reckoned with in politics. One reason for this is found in the size and nature of his party in the Commons. It was just large enough to be of real importance if the Government's position was precarious: it numbered twenty-one in 1741 and more than thirty in 1751. Many of its members held posts in Frederick's Household, and the number which did so increased. This not only distinguished Frederick's party from all other parliamentary groups but also enabled it to cut across them. Between 1737 and 1742, for example, the effectiveness of Frederick's group was born of its juncture with the 'boy patriots', especially with Cobham's Cubs — Pitt and Lyttelton, both members of Frederick's Household, and the two elder Grenvilles — and with the Pulteney and Carteret groups of discontented Whigs. In the background were the Tories, urged by Bolingbroke, constantly but with indifferent success, to join with the independent Whigs. After 1742 Frederick's alliance with Cobham broke down. Frederick's growing support of Carteret, whom he believed 'a man of great ideas in foreign affairs', and his willingness to support a Government of which Carteret was a member, shows some independence of mind. Carteret's fall in November 1744 further separated Frederick from the Cobham group. Lyttelton accepted office as a Junior Lord of the Treasury and Frederick dismissed him from his Household; Pitt resigned in 1745. For Pitt, however, Frederick retained his friendliness and desire that 'when he came to the Crown, Mr. Pitt would continue in his confidence'. Frederick's 'new opposition' in 1747 differed from his earlier opposition, for now the initiative lay with him and he had no Whig allies. Granville was reconciled to Pelham in 1747, Pulteney (now Earl of Bath) stood aloof, the Cobham group was included in Pelham's Government. On the eve of the 1747 elections, therefore, Frederick tried to form an alliance with the Tories. Representatives of his Household met representatives of the Tories and a programme of reforms was devised. Nevertheless, the elections were a triumph for the Government, and Frederick's failures, especially in Cornwall, contrasted sharply with his successes in 1741. In the next year, however, Frederick was successful both in strengthening his party in the Commons and in attracting to it some independent Whigs. In the beginning of 1749 he won a significant victory. Dodington, who had advised Frederick in favour of moderation until 1735 and deserted him in 1737, resigned his post as Treasurer of the Navy in Pelham's Government and became Treasurer of the Chambers in Frederick's Household. Dodington's aim was to persuade Frederick, as Bolingbroke had tried to persuade him earlier, that an alliance with one party was not enough: he must build up a 'national party', and bide his time. For Bolingbroke, the problem had been to broaden the opposition by an alliance with the Tories; now, the problem was to broaden it by an alliance with dissentient Whigs. The task was more difficult than it had been in 1741, for Pelham's policy, unlike Walpole's, was to appease as many as possible of his potential critics by including them in his Government. But perhaps Dodington was right in thinking that, in time, they would leave it and join Frederick, provided Frederick was patient and did not harm his cause by indiscriminate support of the Tories. At any rate, early in 1751 Frederick was approached both by Newcastle, who was threatening to resign from the Cabinet if Bedford was not dismissed, and by his old allies the Cobham group. Frederick's death in March, 1751, therefore hit the 'new opposition' just as it was beginning to show promise of strength. In June, 1751, Pelham felt able safely to dismiss Bedford, for there was now no opposition for him to join.

Frederick's ideas about foreign policy — perhaps the chief factor delineating and dividing parliamentary groups in the generation before and after Walpole's fall — help to explain why he was not continuously in opposition. Something more is needed to explain why, among these groups, Frederick's sympathy lay particularly with the Cobhamites and with the Tories. This was 'patriotism': a group of ideas associated in the 1730s with Wyndham, with Pitt and the 'boy patriots', with the *Craftsman, or Countryman,* and taken up by radicals in the 1760s and by parliamentary reformers in the 1780s. These ideas are inseparably linked with the name of Bolingbroke. Bolingbroke's analysis of politics is found especially in his *Dissertation upon Parties, Remarks on the History of England,* and various papers in the *Craftsman.* It was twofold: he argued that 'Whig' and 'Tory' were outworn labels because the original Whig and Tory principles, operative in 1688, were no longer applicable, and he argued that the 'so-called Whigs' under Walpole kept themselves in power partly by pretending that these labels still had meaning, and partly by what Bolingbroke termed 'corruption'. On this analysis Bolingbroke based his programme. He advocated opposition to Walpole by a 'national party', which should include Tories as well as independent or 'uncorrupted' Whigs and therefore be capable of replacing Walpole's narrow administration by a broadly-based one. This new administration, composed of 'honest men', must then turn to an attack on corruption, with the aim of producing a free and independent House of Commons in place of the existing one, reduced to servility by places and pensions. This attack would be difficult, and would be reinforced if there should arise a good and wise king, willing to renounce corruption and to work with a free Parliament. Indeed, without such a king the attack might well fail. Bolingbroke's analysis of politics appealed to Dodington, who thought it correct; his advocacy of a 'national party' appealed to Wyndham, who wished to modernize the Tories by forcing them to forget Jacobitism; the idea of an attack on corruption appealed to the Tories and to 'patriots'; the idea that a patriot king would support that attack and guarantee its success appealed, amongst others, to Frederick.

The phrase 'patriot king' has often been regarded as a contradiction in terms. The patriot programme meant, in practice, place bills, short parliaments, free elections, the destruction of the king's influence over Parliament. How, it is asked, could a king — or anyone except an opposition — advocate such a programme, or pay more than lip-service to it? Indeed, the programme itself is generally regarded as synonymous with sterile opposition — either unintelligent or insincere — in the sense that what its advocates attacked were, in fact, the very things that made eighteenth-century government work. Although this is true, it ought not to be too readily assumed that these things were indispensable. Here one might consider, as a parallel, the anticipated and the actual effect of the 1832 Reform Act on the working of the constitution. The implementation of the patriot programme might well have resulted, as the Reform Act did, not in making government impossible but in transforming its conventions and so making it work differently. It is true, of course, that many eighteenth-century oppositions adopted something like a patriot programme, and dropped it as soon as they were in office. This perhaps proves, however, not that the programme was misconceived but that, as Bolingbroke knew, politicians are weak and find it difficult when in power to do all they promised in opposition. It was for just this reason that Bolingbroke insisted that the patriot programme might well fail of realization unless it gained a king's support.

It was perhaps unlikely that this would happen. But it was not impossible. Frederick's son, Prince George, found ideas of this kind attractive not only as a way of measuring his grandfather's shortcomings but also as a programme for himself as king. Nor did he drop these ideas as soon as he became King in 1760, though he had little success either in his aim of 'reformation' or in his aim of obtaining a non-party administration. Later, indeed, though not at the time, George III's aims, perhaps deliberately misunderstood, were stigmatized as unconstitutional, the result of arbitrary notions. It does not seem fanciful to suppose that Frederick — whose entry into politics coincided with the *Craftsman*, the 'boy patriots', and the writing of the *Patriot King*, and who bequeathed to George as ministers not only Bute but other members of his Court — would, if he had lived, have forestalled his son and been the first king to try to put patriot ideas into practice. Pitt, after all, praised Frederick as 'most patriot of princes'. William Belsham, writing in 1795, applied the criterion of 'patriotism' to George III's conduct and found it wanting. Frederick, on the other hand, 'so far as the means of judging are afforded to us', wrote Belsham cautiously, 'seems to have been distinguished by the rectitude of his intentions, the generosity and ingenuousness of his conduct. He was desirous to govern the English Nation upon maxims truly English, and was fired with the noble ambition of realizing in his own person that grand and perfect model of a PATRIOT KING, delineated by the happiest effort of transcendant genius.'

IV

The Industrialists

by MICHAEL FLINN

I

THE eighteenth century is a watershed in industrial history: in giving birth to the factory system it divided an era of production in small, scattered units from one of large-scale organization. In cotton spinning the new forms of organization were the outcome of power-driven machinery and the steam engine; in other industries technical advance favoured the increase in the size of the unit of production. But the dramatic social transformation imposed by factory production of textiles has tended to overshadow the continuance, throughout the eighteenth century and in many instances until well into the nineteenth century, of older forms of industrial organization. In most branches of the textile industries outside cotton spinning, and in the finishing branches of the metal trades, the older forms of domestic organization prevailed. On the other hand, in the heavy industries of iron and steel manufacture, shipbuilding, papermaking, and the production of non-ferrous metals, the unit of production had necessarily been relatively large ever since the rise of these industries in the sixteenth century or earlier, and many scores of workers were commonly employed on a single site. The largest industrial units in early eighteenth-century England were probably the naval dockyards of the Thames estuary and the south coast, where the con-

C

struction and repair of ships provided what amounted, in effect, to a partly nationalized industry.

In combination with this variety of forms of industrial organization there was a range of different types of firms in eighteenth-century industry. While some industrialists worked single-handed, others favoured associations in partnerships, companies and even cartels.

Most of the individual industrialists were to be found in small-scale industry, but a few — in many cases those whose names are most familiar — operated on the heroic scale. There were on the one hand men like Peter Stubs, file-maker and inn-keeper of Warrington in the later decades of the century. He employed barely a score of workers both on his own premises and as outworkers. On the other hand were the lone builders of industrial empires like Sir Ambrose Crowley, who in the last years of the seventeenth century and the early years of the eighteenth century founded the largest iron manufacturing business in Europe. His factories in County Durham employed several hundred workmen, while many more found work in warehouses in London and the Midlands, and on board his own fleet of ships.

For the most part, however, the industrialists who worked on their own were to be found in domestic industry. Credit facilities, by permitting the manufacturer to operate on relatively little capital, opened the field to small businesses. Elijah Brooke of Morley is a good example of the small-scale manufacturer common in the Yorkshire woollen industry of the eighteenth century who graduated from worker to employer by these means. After duly serving an apprenticeship, followed by a period as a journeyman in the employment of another clothier, he established his own business in 1780, eventually employing twelve journeymen in addition to members of his own family, some working on his premises, others working in their own homes. In nailmaking, a major industry employing over ten thousand domestic workers in the Black Country, an account of 1775 estimated that there were some fifty nail ironmongers, or nailmasters, the employers of this industry. These men provided the rod iron which was the raw material of the hand-nailers, and marketed the finished product, paying the nailer a piece-rate for his work. The important woollen cloth industry of the West of England and East Anglia was managed by a large number of small employers of this type.

On the other hand, corporate forms of organization were very common in eighteenth-century industry. These took the form of partnerships or companies. They offered the advantages of the spread of risk, access to wider sources of capital, the pooling of technical and commercial skills, and, on occasion, the elimination of undesirable competition. These advantages more than offset the disadvantages of a very imperfect body of company law, and as the century progressed industrialists increasingly turned to partnerships and larger associations as the safest and most efficient forms of organization.

This wide variety in the types of industrial undertaking in the eighteenth century was matched by a comparable breadth of scale. Undertakings ranged from small partnerships like that between James Hargreaves, the inventor of the spinning jenny, and Mr James, a Nottingham joiner, which between 1768 and 1778 operated a small cotton spinning mill in Nottingham, to the vast organization involving capital of almost £200,000 built by the unaided efforts of Sir Ambrose Crowley before his death in 1713; or from the minute Sheffield workshop in which Benjamin Huntsman devised the crucible process of steelmaking in the 1740s with the aid of his three workmen, to the immense copper empire of the late eighteenth century in which Thomas Williams and his partners controlled capital resources of £800,000. Besides the small army of 'domestic' employers in the West of England cloth industry there were men like John Anstie, who at the time of his bankruptcy in 1793 owned ten factories, workshops and fulling mills in and around Devizes, and employed many hundreds of workers. In the metal industries of the Midlands, industrialists like John Taylor, whose metal-ware factory gave employment to five hundred workers, rubbed shoulders with independent craftsmen employing a journeyman and an apprentice or two in backyard workshops.

The scale on which an industrialist operated was determined by the nature of the market for his product — poor communications throughout most of the eighteenth century imposed dispersed rather than concentrated production; and partly by the state of technology — economies of large-scale production were non-existent in most industries, while in some there were positive dis-economies of scale. Very large undertakings were, therefore, exceptional. So long as poor communications imposed geographical limitations on the size of the market of any one producer, the urge to expand the scale of operations, strong in many businessmen, necessarily took the form of the diffusion of interests over a wider range of activities. The Chadwick family, for example, primarily concerned in ironworks in Lancashire in the mid-eighteenth century, was also financially involved in copper mining and smelting, lead mining, and ironworks in Scotland and Wales. Thomas Botfield, whose main interest lay in iron and coal in the late eighteenth century, by the end of the Napoleonic Wars controlled three paper mills in Shropshire. Brewers threw their nets even more widely. Samuel and John Palmer, brewers of Bath, operated two theatres, a tallow

chandler's business and a spermaceti factory, while the
Cobbold family of Ipswich added corn and malt trading,
shipowning and banking to their extensive brewing business.

It was the last of these — banking — which provided
the most important of the diversions of industrialists from
the main stream of industrial development. The eighteenth century laid the foundations of provincial banking
in England, and industry provided a major source of re-
cruitment for bankers. It was a branch of business that
grew naturally from the credit transactions involved in
industrial undertakings. The metal industries gave birth
to many bankers — Sampson Lloyd and John Taylor from
the Birmingham metalware industry; the Walkers of
Rotherham and the Gibbons of Wolverhampton, both
ironmaking families. John Barker of Lichfield and the
Finch family of Dudley, nailmasters, turned from domestic
industry to banking in the late eighteenth century. Several
members of the copper partnerships of the late eighteenth
century entered banking. Thomas Williams with his partner, Edward Hughes, founded the Chester and North
Wales Bank. But it was the brewers, pre-eminently, who
became bankers. Over thirty provincial and ten London
brewers became bankers or entered banking partnerships
in the late eighteenth and early nineteenth centuries; the
list includes names famous in both brewing and banking,
like Greenall, Worthington, Cobbold, Threlfall, Barclay,
Hoare and Gurney.

II

While the unit of industrial organization remained relatively small, the successful industrialist was perforce a man
of many parts. For the work of an industrialist compre-
hended raising capital, organizing a labour force, having

command over the changing techniques of production, organizing the purchase of raw materials and the marketing of the finished product, and — most important in an era of sharp expansion and rapid technical change — perceiving and seizing new openings.

Because of the relatively small scale of industrial equipment in the eighteenth century, the problem of raising capital was seldom an insuperable barrier to enterprise. Capital was required for two purposes — for machines and buildings on the one hand, and to provide stocks of raw materials and to finance the credit essential in the sale of the finished products on the other. In practice the requirements for the latter purpose exceeded by many times those for the former. Surprisingly little capital sufficed in many industries to establish a manufactory. In brewing, £200 would purchase the necessary equipment of a 'common brewhouse'. Many of the metalware manufacturers in eighteenth-century Birmingham began business with less than £100. In 1745, after four years of expansion from humble beginnings, the iron forge of the Walker brothers in Rotherham was valued at only £400. The much heavier demands for 'circulating' capital were more easily met through trade credit and loans from the emerging country banks.

The central problem of raising fixed capital remained, even though the sums involved were not so large. When the needs of capital exceeded the resources available to a single industrialist, the balance had to be raised by partnerships. This was necessary in the eighteenth century because, with only a few exceptions, companies with transferable shares which could be bought and sold in the open market did not exist. An act of 1720 (known, misleadingly, as the 'Bubble Act') had vaguely prohibited unchartered companies, while the absence of an established market for

industrial shares discouraged the development of this
method of finance. In spite of this, companies with transferable shares were not unknown in eighteenth-century
industry, particularly in the copper industry, but several
of these were companies formed before 1720 and were in
any case little more than large partnerships.

Partnerships of perhaps two to six members provided
the principal medium for the mobilization of capital in
eighteenth-century industry. Large sections of the iron
industry were controlled by a relatively small number of
such partnerships. There were, at the one extreme, associations of two or three partners operating a small group
of furnaces and forges like that between Ambrose Crowley,
senior, of Stourbridge, and John Hanbury of Pontypool,
which operated blast furnaces at Treforest and Ynyscedwyn
in South Wales in the early years of the century, and, at
the other extreme, powerful concerns like the interlocking
partnerships by which the Foley, Wheeler, Cotton and
Hall families controlled over fifty furnaces, forges and
slitting mills in the Forest of Dean and the west and north
Midlands in the early eighteenth century. Two similar
groups built the important iron industry of the Furness
district of Lancashire between 1711 and 1750. Well-known
firms like the Darby enterprise at Coalbrookdale in Shropshire, though managed by members of the Darby family,
were in fact owned by partnerships of which the Darbys
were themselves merely members. The famous Carron
works in Scotland, founded in 1759, were the creation of a
partnership consisting of Dr Roebuck, a Birmingham
physician, Samuel Garbett, a Birmingham manufacturer,
and William Cadell, a Scottish merchant. Even in smaller,
more highly localized, industries, partnerships pre-
dominated. The window-glass industry of the early eighteenth century, for example, concentrated in Stourbridge,

was dominated by four family partnerships which, in 1703, signed an agreement that effectively cartelized the industry. And in the silk industry which was beginning to secure a foothold in the North of England in the middle decades of the century, a partnership of six, bringing together landowners and merchants, was instrumental in bringing the factory production of silk thread to Stockport in the 1730s.

So long as the preponderance of wealth lay in the estates of landowners, industrialists seeking capital had to ally themselves with the landed gentry and aristocracy. Richard Knight, a Stour valley ironmaster, for example, raised nearly half the capital for a venture in 1726 to operate the Hales iron furnace in Worcestershire by a partnership with Sir Thomas Lyttelton, lord of the manor of Halesowen. The Backbarrow iron company in the Furness district of Lancashire raised capital in 1715 by means of small loans from a number of local gentry and merchants. The list of members of the landed gentry and aristocracy who invested their accumulated rents in industry in the eighteenth century is a long one: it includes, for example, the Duke of Devonshire who, in the 1790s, poured tens of thousands of pounds into lead mining in the Yorkshire dales; Lord Penrhyn, whose investment from 1765 onwards created the North Wales slate-quarrying industry; and the Earl of Balcarres, whose partnership with the Wigan ironmaster, James Corbett, in 1788, built the Haigh ironworks in south Lancashire.

The industrialists themselves generated much of their own 'fixed' capital. Frugal living permitted the profits of their enterprises to be converted into additional capital. The Walker brothers of Rotherham allowed themselves ten shillings a week each to live on in the early stages of their firm's history. Not until they had been in business for sixteen years and their capital had grown to £7,000 did the brothers allow themselves a dividend of £140 — two per cent. Alternatively, the profits of trade were enlisted for industry. Most of the capital which initiated the famous Darby works at Coalbrookdale in 1708–9 was put up by Bristol merchants, while the capital with which David Dale constructed the famous New Lanark cotton mill in 1786 derived mainly from his profits as an overseas trader.

The management of labour was an art which could make or mar an industrialist. James Whatman gave up his fine Kentish paper-making business in 1793 largely because of the growing difficulties of coping with the demands of labour in a period of acute social unrest: nor was he alone in finding this a major stumbling-block. Industrialists like Sir Ambrose Crowley, who devised an elaborate system of social welfare in his Durham factories in the early eighteenth century with a view to ensuring that his workmen would be 'quiet and easy amongst themselves and a happy and flourishing people amongst their neighbours', or like Robert Owen, who converted the 'very wretched society' of the New Lanark workers into a model village, were shining lights in a dark age. This is not to say that all eighteenth-century industrialists were bad employers. Though few went to the lengths of Crowley or Owen, there were many who strove to create living and working conditions which were often far above the general level of the period. The Quaker, William Champion, who established a large copper and brass works at Warmley near Bristol in 1746, designed an attractive village for his workpeople and devoted much thought and money to the provision of amenities. Lord Penrhyn, the landowning organizer of slate-quarrying in North Wales in the 1770s, arranged a Friendly Society amongst his quarrymen to provide benefits in sickness and old age.

The industrialists who succeeded in establishing happy relations with their workpeople were often those who worked on a large scale. In domestic industry, on the other hand, relations between master and out-worker were seldom happy, while in whole industries like coal-mining, printing and silk manufacture, industrial conflict was endemic throughout the century. In general the wages of all but the most skilled workers permitted only the lowest standard of living, so that higher earnings in booms were too often squandered on drink. There was an almost complete absence of education, and, in all industries that could use it, child labour was the rule. Even a 'good' employer like Jedediah Strutt, one of the first of the cotton-factory employers in the Derbyshire of the 1770s, operated an elaborate system of forfeits for indiscipline amongst his workers. Operatives were fined for such various offences as 'idleness and looking thro' window', 'calling thro' window to some soldiers', 'terrifying S. Pearson with her ugly face', as well as for the more obvious offences of theft, absence and bad work.

Industrialization intensified the class war, yet — or possibly because of this — the eighteenth century saw a decisive change in the attitude of the employing classes to their workers. At least until the mid-eighteenth century the prevailing belief was that the working classes were innately idle, with the result that only low wages would force hard work out of them through sheer necessity of earning a bare living. Perhaps through the experience of a few enlightened employers, there was a reaction from this extreme as the century progressed. It began to be recognized that not all workers were incorrigibly idle and that subsistence wages might in the long run destroy all incentive to effort. 'No society', observed Adam Smith in 1776, 'can surely be flourishing and happy, of which the far greater part of the members are poor and miserable.' Later economists drew attention to the importance of working-class consumption as an element in the demand for the product of industry. But the changed climate of economic thought was slow to affect the attitudes of the vast majority of industrial employers with their noses to the grindstone of profit-making. In spite of earlier examples, New Lanark in the early nineteenth century was still a wonder sufficiently rare to draw astonished visitors from all parts of the world.

The successful management of labour demands the respect of labour, and where skilled work is involved this respect can only be earned by the technical proficiency of the employer himself. In an age of rapid technological advance it was more than ever essential for the industrialist to keep abreast of changing techniques of manufacture. Fortunately, while the scale of industry remained relatively small, this was possible, and the eighteenth-century industrialists excelled as technologists — industrialist and inventor were frequently one and the same man. Sometimes it was an inventor who turned to the organization of production as a means of exploiting his invention, as did William Hargreaves when he established his spinning mill in Nottingham in the 1760s, or Huntsman when he gave up watchmaking to become a steelmaker after his discovery of the crucible process in 1740; but, more commonly, technical progress emerged from the intense preoccupation of the industrialists themselves with the actual process of manufacture. Abraham Darby was a practising ironmaster whose discovery of coke-smelting early in the century primarily enabled him to cut his costs. Isaac, the father of the better-known John Wilkinson, himself an ironmaster on a modest scale, took out several patents for improved methods of production. James Whatman. the owner of a large paper-mill near Maidstone, developed as a result of his own researches a technique for the production of fine paper in sheets of unprecedented size, to earn the gratitude of printers and engravers. These are merely a few examples from a long list of industrialists — men like Cort, Arkwright, Lombe and Strutt — whose inventions contributed to the Industrial Revolution.

Though less dramatic than invention and less fundamental than the provision of capital and labour, a mastery of commercial organization was nonetheless an essential item in the equipment of an industrialist. As the historian of the English brewing industry has recently emphasized, 'in no quarter could disaster come more quickly than from inefficient buying'. This aspect has not, until recently, received much attention from historians, yet in a century of expanding industry the problems attached to the supply of raw materials and the sale and distribution of the finished products were assuming greater importance, relatively as well as absolutely. In practice, of course, these problems filled a greater part of the industrialist's working day than all the others put together. Only the woollen industry could be said to have any effective regional marketing organization, in the 'cloth halls' of the West Riding towns, at Shrewsbury, Norwich, and, above all, at Blackwell Hall in London. The Liverpool raw cotton market, the Manchester cotton exchange, the Glasgow pig iron market and the London commodity exchanges, with their elaborate though valuable devices of 'futures' dealings, did not emerge until the nineteenth century. With nothing of this kind to facilitate his task, the eighteenth-century industrialist stood to lose all if he failed in these directions.

The partnership, indeed, was a device for solving some of these problems. Partners were taken on because of their connections with the supply of a raw material. This led to extensive vertical integration by which partnerships of industrialists, each primarily concerned with one process, extended their control over the whole range of production. This was particularly frequent in the iron industry, while in the copper industry of the late eighteenth century Thomas Williams succeeded for a brief period in building an organization which integrated and monopolized the whole field of copper manufacture from the ore to the final product. In the absence of direct integration of this kind, family relationships filled the need. The Quakers, whose industrial strength was out of all proportion to their numbers, inter-married extensively, and used their marriage ties to further the interests of business.

The problem of finding outlets for the finished products was handled in a variety of ways. Just as partnerships were sometimes a means of raising capital, so could they be used to market the manufactured products. Thus the same Bristol merchants who subscribed capital to the Coalbrookdale enterprise bought a part of its output for disposal overseas or by coastal navigation to other parts of the country. In industries like ship-building, iron-making and brewing, for which the navy was a major customer, industrialists went to immense lengths to secure and retain contracts. Indeed, the need to maintain close relations with the fount of custom was a principal factor behind the entry into Parliament of naval contractors like Sir Ambrose Crowley (iron), Sir John Parsons (brewing) or Sir Henry Johnson (shipbuilding). The eighteenth century saw the effective beginning, though on the smallest of scales, of advertising by manufacturers in the Press. In the last resort, however, it was personal contact that won and retained markets, and the eighteenth-century industrialist was not afraid to take to the road. Fothergill, Matthew Boulton's early partner, travelled extensively in Europe, particularly in the Baltic area, in search of custom, while in the 1750s Jedediah Strutt, a hosiery manufacturer of Derby, took samples of his own speciality, ribbed hose, personally to London, where the principal hosiery buyers were concentrated. William Playne, woollen manufacturer of Longford, Gloucestershire, used to keep a carriage and horses permanently at Calais in readiness for his annual commercial visits to the Continent.

Finally, the business of the industrialist without imagination, without an eye for opportunity, was inevitably condemned to stagnation. It was not merely a question of anticipating changes in consumers' tastes or needs, of calculating the implication of changes in prices of raw materials, or of speculating on future trends of raw material or finished product prices. The industrialist who made good was the one who, in addition, foresaw the economic possibilities of new techniques. Josiah Wedgwood, for example, succeeded partly because he followed to their logical conclusion Adam Smith's principles of the division of labour; John Wilkinson, because he devised a new application of power when he harnessed the steam pump to the blast furnace in 1776; the Darbys, because they realised that Newcomen's steam pump created a valuable market for cast-iron cylinders; Sir Thomas Lombe, because he triumphed in the quest for a silk-throwing machine which could be effectively used in large-scale production. Almost every successful industrialist in the eighteenth century, as in any other century, made good because he detected new economic openings. To grasp these opportunities required courage, imagination and self-confidence; but unless these qualities were accompanied by the ability to raise capital, manage labour, control a commercial organization, and above all to get on with partners, disaster was inevitable.

III

What sort of people were the industrialists? Where did they come from? How did they train themselves? What sort of lives did they live? What use did they make of the power their wealth brought them? These and many similar questions open up immense avenues to historical exploration. They produce an infinite variety of answers which exemplify the rich diversity of human nature to be found amongst the industrial tycoons of the eighteenth century.

Their social origins, for example, embrace the whole range of social strata. Many successful manufacturers graduated from the ranks of the artisans, for this class enjoyed the inestimable advantage of technical skill without which no business could succeed. It is not surprising to find, therefore, that the institution of apprenticeship threw up many men of outstanding quality. John Taylor, for example, the founder with Sampson Lloyd of a famous bank in 1765, who employed five hundred men making metal wares in his Birmingham workshop and left a fortune of nearly a quarter of a million pounds, began his working life as a cabinet-maker's apprentice. Other industrialists whose early apprenticeship in a skilled craft paved the way to industrial fame include William Cookworthy, who walked to London from Devon at the age of thirteen in 1719 to take up an apprenticeship with an apothecary, and who later discovered and exploited the Cornish china clay deposits; David Dale, who began as a Paisley weaver and ended as a cotton magnate; James Haggas, bound apprentice to a Halifax worsted weaver in 1715, who within twenty years had built up a business capable of producing several hundred cloths weekly; and a host of well-known manufacturers whose names include

Jedediah Strutt, Richard Arkwright, Samuel Oldknow, Abraham Darby and Samuel Garbett.

At the other end of the social scale, wealth generated by land offered an obvious *entrée* into industry. The Earl of Balcarres, the Duke of Devonshire, and Lord Penrhyn, already mentioned, were carrying on a well-established tradition in exploiting the mineral wealth of their lands. They were followed by other landowners, small men as well as big. Sir Humphry Mackworth, owner of extensive estates in South Wales, engaged in a number of ventures in coal, copper, tin and silver mining, albeit with little financial success. Several of the Furness ironmasters were medium landowners of that district. John Chadwick, an ironmaster of early eighteenth-century Lancashire on a modest scale, had begun as a yeoman farmer, while the first Samuel Whitbread, founder of a great brewing house, came of good yeoman stock in Bedfordshire.

It was the middle class, rather than the working class or the landed gentry or aristocracy, that provided the solid core of the eighteenth-century industrial class. Professional life not infrequently provided the contacts that led to active participation in industry. The 'copper king', Thomas Williams, was an Anglesey lawyer whose professional dealings introduced him to the groups interested in exploiting the copper deposits re-discovered there in the 1760s. One of his partners in these ventures was the Reverend Edward Hughes, a country parson whose marriage brought him part-ownership of some of the copper-bearing land. Another of Williams' associates, Sir Charles Roe, was the son of a Derbyshire parson. Yet another parson to turn to industry was the Reverend Edmund Cartwright, brother of the Radical politician, Major Cartwright, and inventor of the power-loom. Having successfully applied a power-drive to the loom, he decided to go into power-weaving himself, and in 1787 set up two small factories in Don-caster for that purpose. It was to be expected that trade would lead to industry, and not a few traders followed mer-chant capital into industry. William Cadell, one of the three founders of the Carron ironworks, was a merchant, as were both Anthony Bacon and Richard Crawshay, founders of the great Cyfarthfa ironworks in South Wales in the 1760s.

With the expansion of the scale of industry during the eighteenth century a professional managerial class emerged. In the iron and brewing industries some extremely com-petent and influential salaried managers appeared. Crow-ley's manager in the 1730s, John Bannister, was widely consulted by the government on questions concerning trade policy. He drew a salary of £500 per annum, while the managers of some of the larger London breweries achieved as much as £1,000 per annum by the end of the century. Not surprisingly, some of these officials themselves became entrepreneurs. William Balston, who started in 1774 as apprentice to the Kentish paper-maker, James Whatman, and rose to a senior clerkship, became a mem-ber (with capital lent by Whatman) of the partnership which bought his flourishing business twenty years later. In 1782 the last of a long succession of managers, Isaiah Mil-lington, bought a share in the huge Crowley business from the Earl of Ashburnham, who had acquired it through marriage. Millington and his descendants assumed absolute control of the business for the remaining eighty years of its existence. The death of the London brewer, Henry Thrale, in 1781, without a male heir, allowed John Perkins, for twenty years his manager, to take over his business in partnership with Robert Barclay of the wealthy Quaker banking family.

An American historian has recently drawn attention to

the fact that many of the great American industrialists of the nineteenth century were not, as is so often thought, entirely self-made men. Most of them had their feet firmly placed on the first, or even second, rung of the ladder by their fathers. This is also very true of English industrialists in the eighteenth century. Some of the very greatest of the makers of the Industrial Revolution got off to a flying start in this way. John Wilkinson's father was a well-established ironmaster; Matthew Boulton, the partner of James Watt, got his first introduction to industry in the flourishing business operated by his father in Birmingham.

Relatively few industrialists enjoyed the benefits of formal schooling. Education was not generally available to the working class, while the classical grounding offered to the middle class by the average grammar or private school was of little value to the aspiring industrialist. It was the dissenting academies of the North of England which, by virtue of their advanced curricula stressing science, mathematics and accounting, were the most valuable nurseries of industrialists. John Wilkinson had attended Dr Caleb Rotheram's Dissenting Academy at Kendal in the 1740s, while his younger brother, William, who was to make his mark in French industry, was sent to Dr Joseph Priestley's school at Nantwich, Cheshire. Industrialists with the benefit of a university education were rare, for only the Scottish universities provided an education in the eighteenth century which could be regarded in any sense as a preparation for the world of industry. The scientific background acquired in the study of medicine at Edinburgh led Dr Roebuck through industrial chemistry into industry itself, while the same medical school produced James Keir, the Midlands glass-maker of the later eighteenth century who turned to the large-scale manufacture of chemicals at the famous Tipton Alkali Works.

It was no coincidence that industrialists and the sons of industrialists received their education at dissenting academies; there was a strong connection between industry and Dissent, and amongst the Dissenters the Quakers in particular were pre-eminent. The ranks of the Quakers at this time were recruited, unlike those of the Anglicans, the Methodists and the Catholics, very largely from the industrial and commercial middle class as well as from the higher grades of skilled craftsmen. In Quaker circles craftsmen like Abraham Darby graduated very naturally to the ranks of the employers. The eighteenth-century Quakers married mostly within the Society of Friends; their system of monthly, quarterly and yearly meetings drew together convocations of businessmen with similar interests, so that the tightly-knit bonds of Quaker industrial society promoted the welfare of both counting-house and meeting-house. The iron industry was dominated by Quaker groups in Shropshire, the Midlands, south Yorkshire and Furness, and the inter-relationship of these Quaker groups — which included the Darby, Crowley, Lloyd, Cotton, Fell, Rawlinson, Reynolds, Hanbury, Pemberton and Parkes families — amounted, in effect, almost to cartelization of the industry.

Why was there such a strong connection between industrial management and nonconformity, particularly Quakerism? Since the appeal of Quakerism was confined to a fairly narrow section of the social hierarchy, and since some professional and political avenues were closed to Dissenters, Quakers were artificially concentrated in the field of industrial and commercial management. But the secret of their success lay more in their attitude to their working life. Believing fanatically in the virtues of hard work, honesty and sobriety, as well as in the need for straightforward dealing and plain humanity in their relations with each other and with their workpeople, they avoided excessive risk and combined persistent vigour with cautious enterprise. It was a recipe for modest progress rather than dramatic expansion, and explains, at least in part, why so many Quaker industrialists ended their careers as bankers.

The new men of the Industrial Revolution have so often been portrayed as brash, ignorant *nouveaux riches* that it comes rather as a pleasant surprise to find that, in fact, a great many of them were men of taste, elegance and culture. They were present everywhere in the sprouting scientific, philosophical and statistical societies which signified the age's new-found interest in intellectual discussion. Dr Johnson, 'bustling about with an ink-horn and pen in his button hole, like an excise man', was by no means out of place in Henry Thrale's brewery counting-house. The wealth acquired in industry was not infrequently devoted to cultural ends. One of Erard's first pianofortes went in 1786 to Samuel Oldknow, 'packed up very carefully', as his London agent wrote him, 'by Pickford's wagon — I hope you will find sweet music in it that will wrap your soul as Milton says in Elizium'. James Whatman, the paper-maker, was a collector of paintings, and, indeed, a great many industrialists patronized the arts at least to the extent of commissioning portraits of themselves and their families by such artists as Romney or Joseph Wright of Derby. Part of Wedgwood's success is due to the very high artistic taste of his pottery designs.

Not unnaturally the scientific strain outweighed the artistic in the eighteenth-century industrialists, for in this sphere a spirit of enquiry blended happily with self-interest. Midland engineers, Lancashire textile finishers, and chemical manufacturers everywhere, were keenly preoccupied with scientific study and research. Nor were their enquiries confined to their own narrow fields. James

Watt was actively interested in the search for a synthetic alkali, and Josiah Wedgwood and Matthew Boulton in the development of accurate scientific instruments. This disinterested enthusiasm of the industrialists of the later eighteenth century for the advance of pure science has led a distinguished historian to assert recently that the Industrial Revolution was fundamentally an intellectual movement. Perhaps the most striking manifestation of this trend was the Lunar Society in Birmingham. This society, so called because its evening meetings were held for convenience monthly at the full moon, was an informal gathering of Birmingham scientists and industrialists for the discussion of whatever scientific and philosophical problems interested them.

Other industrialists concerned themselves more broadly with the general welfare of the society in which they lived. There were those like Sir Ambrose Crowley, Samuel Oldknow or Robert Owen, who devoted immense thought and resources to the creation of civilized communities for their workpeople. The Strutts, on the other hand, did much to embellish the town of Derby with bridges, paving, lighting, hospitals, schools and churches. It would be as improper to place responsibility for the urban squalor of the nineteenth century at the feet of individual industrialists as it would be to hold the physicists of a later age responsible for the threat of nuclear war in the twentieth century. Both groups are mere participants, albeit willingly, in economic or political systems.

IV

Throughout this essay the eighteenth century has been treated as a homogeneous whole, no distinction having been made for the most part between industrialists of the earlier and later parts of the century. Yet there were clearly momentous developments in English industry during the century, producing industrial conditions in 1800 which differed dramatically from those of 1700. How far did this mean that the industrialists of the 'Industrial Revolution' differed from their fellows of a calmer age?

This is a difficult question to answer. Few of the fundamental factors which determined the status of the industrialist changed. There was no real change in the legal structure of business organization which would, for example, breed a new class of professional managers, as did the limited liability legislation of the nineteenth century. Nor were the rewards of successful enterprise necessarily smaller in the earlier period than in the later. The contrasts of barbarity and humanity in labour relations were as sharp in 1700 as in 1800. The accident of history, through the greater survival of business records of the later period, has directed a more powerful searchlight on the behaviour and attitudes of the later generations, with the result that the industrialists of the later eighteenth century have been thrown into sharper relief. The problem is whether this altered perspective conceals or reveals a real change of character.

There were some differences. It is no accident that the 1780s saw the first serious attempts by industrialists to organize themselves for political ends. The General Chamber of Manufacturers of Great Britain, an association of manufacturers of cotton, iron and pottery of 1785, exerted vigorous though only partially effective pressure on the economic policy of Pitt's government in defence of what they believed to be their own long-term interests; for the industrialists had by this time grown sufficiently in number and economic power to constitute for the first time an influential element in the country. The parliaments of Queen Anne contained few industrialists; by the 1840s the 'industrial interest', typified and led by the Manchester cotton manufacturer, Richard Cobden, was able for the first time in history to win a decisive victory over the 'landed interest'.

The new strength of the manufacturers reflected, of course, the wider economic opportunities of the later age. The industrialists themselves had little or no control over the population growth, the expanding overseas markets, the improved communications, the increased agricultural productivity, or the new banking facilities which were the pre-conditions or causes of industrial growth. The role of the industrialists was to relate technological developments to this changing economic background and to grasp opportunities as they presented themselves. In this they succeeded to a remarkable degree, but in the later eighteenth century they were operating in a very different economic environment. If technology, in the shape of the achievements of Cort, Watt or Crompton, presented them with new possibilities of large-scale production, the transport engineers simultaneously laid down the means of fetching and carrying the vastly increased quantities of industrial materials, the banks canalized the nation's savings into industrial investment, and a fortuitous and unexpected population 'explosion' conveniently created an army of industrial labourers. Naturally, the industrialists gave a helping hand to some of these developments — they were behind almost every canal company and turnpike trust of the eighteenth century, for example. But it remains true that circumstances favoured the industrialists of the later part of the century in a way that would have evoked the envy of their predecessors.

It was not, in other words, the actors who had changed, but the scenery. A new backdrop had been lowered and the footlights brightened, but the actors were still trained in the same schools. The Arkwrights, Boultons and Wilkinsons of the last quarter of the century stemmed from much the same origins as the Lombes, Darbys and Lloyds of the first quarter, and grappled with much the same kind of problems. Historical research is gradually revealing a wealth of industrialists of the early eighteenth century as stimulating in personality and originality as those who built on their foundations in the Industrial Revolution. When this work is completed, the continuity and homogeneity of eighteenth-century industrial history will be more firmly established.

SUGGESTIONS FOR FURTHER READING

Unwin, G. & others, *Samuel Oldknow and the Arkwrights*, Manchester University Press, 1924.

Ashton, T. S., *Iron and Steel in the Industrial Revolution*, Manchester University Press, 1924.

―― *The Industrial Revolution*, Home University Library, 1948.

Raistrick, A., *Quakers in Science and Industry*, Bannisdale Press, 1950.

Fitton, R. S. & Wadsworth, A. P., *The Strutts and the Arkwrights, 1758–1830*, Manchester University Press, 1958.

Mathias, P., *The Brewing Industry in England, 1700–1830*, Cambridge University Press, 1959.

V

The Slave Traffic

by J. D. HARGREAVES

IN the twentieth century the African slave-trade is commonly a subject for moral judgments: to Europeans a source of shame and guilt, to Africans, of bitterness and anger. (This anger often reflects genuine personal feeling, for the trade is often and reasonably blamed for the technical backwardness of modern Africa.) For most of the eighteenth century, however, the question was discussed primarily in economic terms (just as nuclear warfare today seems to many honest men a purely military question). Traders and mercantilist writers in Europe shared with West Indian planters the clear conviction that trading in slaves was 'very advantageous to Great Britain, and necessary to the plantations'. Even Africans, at least in those states near the coast which prospered on the profits of selling men, might share this opinion. A historian may feel little initial sympathy for these people; but pronouncing judgment upon their morality is not his main task. He must rather try to understand what purposes they believed the trade was serving, and consider how far their belief was really justified.

Slavery — the relationship in which one person is legally recognized as the property of another — seems to have played some part in the early development of most organized societies; and whenever slaves are regarded at all generally as a marketable commodity a slave-trade may be said to exist. But when *the* slave-trade is referred to, with the definite article, what is commonly meant is the export of West African slaves to the American continent or the Caribbean islands in the period between about 1510 and 1865. This trade is especially important, and especially controversial, firstly because of its magnitude, secondly because it formed an integral part of a very widespread network of commercial relationships.

Negro slaves were first systematically shipped to the Americas early in the sixteenth century; Spanish colonists, where the native population was too scanty or too recalcitrant to provide labour for their mines and farms, bought Africans from Portuguese or other merchants licensed by the Crown — or from illicit traders. At first, the numbers required were not large, possibly averaging nine thousand a year through the sixteenth century. But they increased rapidly as more European colonists settled in the American tropics and began to produce commercial crops on a fairly large scale, in plantations which required a substantial initial investment and the regular services of a considerable unskilled labour force. In the seventeenth century some colonies used European labour extensively — transported convicts or indentured servants; but by the eighteenth most plantations found Negro slaves more economical as a labour force, and easier to control. Crops raised on such plantations included tobacco, rice and indigo; but until the nineteenth century, when industrial growth in Europe multiplied the demand for American cotton, the most important one was sugar.

Spaniards were producing sugar in the West Indies with Negro slaves from about 1508, and the Portuguese grew it on a larger scale in Brazil; but after about 1640 it was progressively introduced into islands more recently settled by English and French colonists, where it became the staple crop. In sugar plantations, Negro slaves were soon exclusively employed for the heavy work of planting, for weeding and trimming the canes, for manuring and digging drainage trenches, and for cutting canes at harvest-time. Often they were used also for more skilled and specialized jobs about the house or plantation — as building tradesmen, in the seasonal work of grinding and boiling, even in such responsible roles as that of head boiler. And of course there were all manner of general duties to be performed; so long as unpaid labour is plentiful, there will always be jobs to be done. By the eighteenth century the prosperity of the European colonies in the Caribbean, and of many of the tropical mainland settlements, depended — or so their influential citizens were unanimously convinced — on a regular and continuing supply of slaves from Africa. And since European governments by now regarded these colonies as essential foundations of their economic prosperity and national power, the slave-trade acquired a distinctive importance to 'mercantilist' theorists and statesmen in Europe.

The usual pattern of the trade was triangular, though many slave-ships followed different routes, taking in both West Indian and mainland ports, or sailing directly between the Americas and Africa. Normally a ship left Europe with a cargo of textiles and miscellaneous goods, carefully assorted to suit the known tastes of African consumers in the area of destination. Five weeks' sailing at least was usually needed from London to the Gambia, much more to distant African ports. Once on the coast, it might take several months to buy a full cargo of slaves (a 'full cargo', very roughly and generally, seems to have been represented by two slaves per ton burden). This process involved much hard bargaining with African suppliers.

Where the slaves originally came from remains uncertain. Many were prisoners of war, and there were numerous instances of African peoples initiating military operations against their neighbours for the express purpose of obtaining saleable prisoners. How general this was it is difficult to say. Other slaves were kidnapped by African entrepreneurs; many were law-breakers, transported by their rulers for murder, adultery or witchcraft; a considerable number were sold for debt. No numerical classification in terms of cause of enslavement or area of origin has yet been attempted. But by the eighteenth century organized arrangements had clearly been made in many parts of West Africa for regular supplies of slaves to African dealers at the coast.

The methods by which Europeans dealt with these African brokers varied regionally. Between the Rio Grande and Cape Mount, slaves were supplied to the ships chiefly by European or mulatto agents, who lived sparsely dispersed through the principal estuaries. Nicholas Owen, an Irishman struggling to re-establish his family fortunes, resided in the Sherbro from 1754 until 1759 in almost complete isolation; 'if it wasn't for my woman and 4 or 5 people,' he wrote, 'I might very well pass for an hermit.' His diary records no transaction involving more than five slaves. To complete a cargo by purchasing from such sources clearly demanded time and patience. Between Cape Mount and the Gold Coast forts there were few European residents. Passing ships signalled their arrival to African towns, canoes came out across the surf, and bargaining took place on shipboard. With no fixed investment on these shores, lawless captains saw nothing to lose, and occasionally acquired slaves by abduction; but this was generally disapproved as liable to give traders of the nation a bad name, and to spoil future business.

These areas were of relatively small importance in the slave-trade. In the Senegal, Gambia, Grande and Sierra Leone rivers, at Whydah, in parts of Angola, and especially on the Gold Coast, trade was based upon permanent European forts or settlements, whose residents aimed to secure regular supplies of slaves and produce, where possible by some quasi-contractual relationship with the local people. But many of these forts had been sited in earlier periods with a view to buying gold rather than slaves, and supplies were often scarce; agents had to go out in search of business, cruising in small coastal craft or establishing 'factories' on the neighbouring coast. (At Whydah, however, a generally good supply of slaves and an efficient marketing organization were provided by the local African authorities.) Gradually the emphasis, of British traders at least, moved westwards, to the Niger delta and the neighbouring rivers. But here the keen and intelligent African exporters were too wary of Europeans to welcome permanent establishments on shore, while the traders found business too good to be left for occasional visits. Eventually a solution was found by the use of hulks, old sea-going ships permanently moored in the river as off-shore trading stations. By the end of the century these methods had made 'the Bights' the greatest slave market in Africa. Captain Adams estimated the port of Bonny alone to be exporting 20,000 slaves a year: doubtless an exaggeration, but not a wild one.

Contrary to a common opinion, slave-dealing in Africa did not necessarily create racial arrogance; this was an attitude more characteristic of the plantations. The essential feature of all transactions on the coast was that Europeans bargained for slaves with other Africans, and they did not always play the dominant role. The tastes of African consumers determined what goods had to be supplied

(150 different lines were needed on the Gold Coast alone, according to Bosman); the bargaining ability of African middlemen determined prices; African rulers provided the security which was needed along the inland trade-routes and at the coastal markets, and insisted on visiting traders complying with prescribed rules and procedures. Nothing could be further from the truth than to imagine the sea-captains dictating the conditions of trade; more often it was the Africans who did this, and the Europeans could resist them only by enlisting the support of a hostile faction or people. But for traders who sought permanent markets in Africa, encouragement of violence and lawlessness was rarely the best policy. The ideal slaver was a patient and tolerant man, with, John Snow advised in 1705,

> good sence & good nature enough as will teach him how to manage people that are not so nice but would be glad to be courted with a kindness very dunstable [straightforward].

And though in African conditions many traders inevitably became irritable and contemptuous, some at least enquired sympathetically into African society. Thomas Phillips judged even the slaves,

> poor creatures, who, excepting their want of Christianity and true religion (their misfortune more than fault) are as much the work of God's hands, and no doubt as dear to him as ourselves; nor can I imagine why they should be despised for their colour, being what they cannot help.

Curious though it may sound, the slave-trade created on parts of the African coast a commercial society in which European and African businessmen uneasily shared common interests.

Once the cargo was complete the Atlantic crossing or 'Middle Passage' began; a period of anxiety for the crew, and of bewildered misery for the slaves, who spent most of the voyage cramped, sometimes physically crushed one against another, between the low slave decks. Usually, though not always, they were kept in irons. This was the aspect of the slave-trade to which the Abolitionists of the later eighteenth century gave most publicity, and some historians have wondered whether their strictures may not have been exaggerated. It is probably true that the financial interest of the captains in reducing losses at sea usually ensured some bare minimum of food, hygiene and medical attention for the slaves, and meant that they were brutally handled only when cruelty was judged essential for the maintenance of discipline; and certainly the treatment of the slaves seems less atrocious when compared with, say, working conditions in eighteenth-century British coal-mines than when judged by modern standards. Even so, attempting to justify the Middle Passage is not a very fruitful use of scholarly energy.

After a voyage of around eight weeks, varying according to destination and weather, the slave-ships reached West Indian or American ports. The slaves, fed and doctored for the occasion, were sold to the planters, usually by auction. Sometimes a return cargo of sugar, tobacco, or cotton was purchased for the owners and taken on board, but very often it was not worth waiting for this and the ship returned in ballast, or carrying freights for other merchants. By the time the vessel returned to its home port, it would have been absent about a year: sometimes less, but often very much more.

The costs of the initial cargo, of shipping, of shore establishments in Africa, demanded the investment of considerable capital. The ultimate return might or might not be generous, but the risk was heavy, and any return inevitably slow. In the seventeenth century few individuals could find long-term capital on such a scale. Yet success in the slave-trade could bring many advantages to the state, according to contemporary economic doctrines: it could stimulate ocean shipping, increase exports to Africa, and perhaps provide a means of entering the coveted markets of Spanish America. So from an early stage governments encouraged their subjects to organize themselves to enter this trade. The Dutch, whose West India Company of 1621 represented the first sustained and successful challenge to the monopolistic claims of Spain and Portugal in the Atlantic, well understood the importance of the slave-trade in their struggle for maritime power. Soon other peoples, including Swedes, Danes, and Brandenburgers, joined in the competition with government support.

For the English and French, with their growing Caribbean colonies, as for the Portuguese in Brazil, the desire to be independent of foreign suppliers of labour provided an additional compulsive reason for fostering the national slave-trade. But trading and planting interests did not necessarily coincide; planters wanted preferential supplies of African labour, while the traders might see more profit in selling slaves to foreign customers. Such a conflict could ultimately be resolved only by governmental policy. So the organization and direction of the slave-trade might be the subject of keen political controversy.

English companies were granted Charters by the Crown for trade in Africa in 1588, 1618, and 1660; but even the latest of this series, the Royal Adventurers into Africa, was poorly organized and short of capital. It was wound up in 1672, when a new Royal Charter, excluding other English subjects from trade in West Africa, was granted to the Royal African Company. This was a London joint-stock company, supported largely by merchants or financiers already established in other business enterprises, and initially by some prominent courtiers and public men. The Stuarts took a keen personal interest, and until 1688 James II, as Duke of York and as King, was its Governor — by no means a purely honorary position. The Company's purpose was to make profits; but it would also have to justify its monopoly by promoting the national commerce and providing slave labour to the English plantations.

Although the Company paid dividends until 1692 at an average annual rate of about 7 per cent, its financial position was never strong, and it was already accumulating heavy debts. Its initial capital of £110,000 proved insufficient, given the slow rate of turnover. Even when a voyage was successfully completed, the return due to the Company might not be quickly negotiable; many West Indian planters had to demand credit for their purchases of slaves, and their debts often proved irrecoverable. There were other risks, too, beyond the normal dangers of shipwreck on the African coast or in a Caribbean hurricane; a cargo of slaves might be decimated by sickness, or lost by mutiny. During most of the Company's life foreign war multiplied the danger of losses at sea, and so increased the cost of shipping charges.

On top of these hazards, inherent in the slave-trade, the Company had, by the terms of its monopoly, to carry overhead expenses by maintaining the English forts in West Africa. They owned altogether eleven of these, built by the Company or its predecessors, or acquired from foreign states: one each on the Gambia, Sierra Leone, and Sherbro rivers, seven in the Gold Coast, and one at Whydah. The strength of the Company's European establishment at these forts — commercial agents, artisans, and soldiers — varied considerably, but at times exceeded three hundred, with African employees in addition; the

D

total cost of manning and maintaining them was about £20,000 a year. Whether the Company benefited in proportion is extremely doubtful. In theory, the forts attracted African dealers and brokers, permitting the Company to buy slaves or gold at all seasons, without waiting for ships; on the other hand, when no slaves were available locally, they represented a commitment which made it harder to switch activities elsewhere. Even militarily they could be a liability; they might involve their occupants in local quarrels, which sometimes ended with Africans occupying the forts, for the actual fortifications were often weak, and directed towards the sea rather than the land. Their main purpose was to uphold the national trade against European competitors: not necessarily by fighting — at Whydah, the English, French and Dutch forts seem to have observed a local truce throughout the war of Spanish Succession — but by providing physical gages for a local balance of power. In effect, the Royal African Company was paying for its monopoly by assuming a share of national military expenditure.

This did not prove a good bargain. Even before 1688 the Company suffered from the intrusion of interlopers from London, the outports, or the British West Indies. These unlicensed traders often benefited from the presence of English forts without contribution to their upkeep: their total share in the slave-trade may have begun to approach the scale of the Company's own. After the Revolution the Company was still less able to enforce a monopoly which rested solely on a Stuart charter, and prepared to compromise with its competitors by issuing an increasing number of licences to 'separate traders'. But it faced increasing pressure, through Parliament, from those who wished to see its monopoly destroyed. These included, besides the rival traders themselves, manufacturers and merchants who believed an open trade would provide a larger market in Africa for English exports, and West Indian and American planters, complaining that the monopolist on whom they depended for their labour supplied too few slaves too dearly. In 1698 Parliament enacted a temporary compromise; all English subjects were free to engage in the West African trade, but for thirteen years an export duty of 10 per cent, and certain import duties on African produce, were to go to the Company, to provide for the upkeep of the forts. Competing under these new conditions, and under the added difficulties of war, the Company's position continued to deteriorate until the remnants of its privileges expired in 1712.

Thereafter, with the trade open to all British subjects on equal terms, the Company continued to decline, though with occasional ephemeral revivals. Until 1730 it attempted to maintain the forts out of its own resources, since abandoning them would have removed the main asset from its balance-sheet; after 1730 Parliament began to vote the Company subsidies for the purpose, usually of £10,000 a year. But leadership in the slave-trade was rapidly passing from London to the outports — first Bristol, then Liverpool. In 1750 this change was recognized when Parliament set up a regulated company — the Company of Merchants Trading to Africa — which took over the forts and other assets of the Royal African Company in 1752. Membership was open to all, on payment of forty shillings; the Company's main income came from a Parliamentary grant, which rose from £10,000 to £23,000 by 1807; its primary duty was to administer the forts, and it was prohibited from corporate trading. This measure did not represent much change in the organization of the African trade, but simply a more equitable method of financing some of its overheads: the government accepted on a permanent basis the financial responsibility for the forts, which it had actually carried since 1730, but avoided extending its political or administrative commitments.

The new company did not play any important role in expanding the slave-trade; from time to time it came under criticism for being oligarchically or restrictively run, or for allowing too much private trade to its employees in the forts. But the bulk of the great eighteenth-century expansion of the slave-trade took place away from the forts, and through the enterprise of individual traders. Precise figures are hard to come by, but those available show British exports to Africa growing from perhaps £100,000 a year in the later seventeenth century to an annual average of over £700,000 in the years 1784-90. This represents a rise from something under 3 per cent to about 4½ per cent of the growing volume of exports. An increasing proportion of these goods was being exchanged for slaves. It has been estimated that the Royal African Company drew perhaps 40 per cent of its income from direct imports of African produce into Britain; but in 1784-90 the declared value of British imports from Africa was only 13 per cent of the value of exports to Africa, which suggests that up to 90 per cent of the goods sent to Africa were being exchanged for slaves. Estimates of the number of slaves thus purchased are also difficult to substantiate. Over the forty years 1672-1711 the Royal African Company delivered over 100,000 slaves alive in the British West Indies, and its private British competitors may well have exceeded this number. The grand total of all European landings of slaves in the Americas during the seventeenth century has been estimated — very roughly — at 2,750,000. But by the 1780s the total of European landings was probably 70,000 or more each year. British ships, now mostly from Liverpool, were carrying something like one half of this total.

This great development of the British slave-trade was welcomed almost unanimously by politicians and publicists, who saw in it 'an inexhaustible Fund of Wealth and Naval Power to this Nation'. Such enthusiasm often seems disproportionate, since exports to tropical Africa formed so small a part of Britain's foreign trade — only about half the direct trade with the British West Indies. A number of branches of the textile and hardware industries did find African markets of some marginal importance; but East Indian textiles were long more popular than British, and even at the end of the eighteenth century only two-thirds of British exports to Africa were manufactured at home. Yet still British leadership in the slave-trade was regarded as a major national interest. Parliament was even willing to encourage the sale of slaves to French and Spanish customers at the expense of English planters (whose interest lay not only in obtaining labour for themselves, but in denying supplies to foreign rivals who might use them to develop new and more productive plantations for sugar). The famous *Asiento* — the contract to supply 4,800 slaves annually, which was secured for the South Sea Company by the Treaty of Utrecht in 1713 — though it proved a disappointing prize and its value is often exaggerated, was bitterly resented by slave-hungry planters in Jamaica. Nevertheless, by the later eighteenth century the purchase and re-export of Negroes in the British West Indies was a flourishing subsidiary branch of the slave-trade.

It is not easy to estimate exactly how profitable the slave-trade really was to individuals or to the nation. One difficulty is that we do not have sufficient sets of well-kept accounts. In those we have, there is the problem of isolating slaving from other business; captains might use a substantial part of their cargo to buy ivory or other African produce, or swell the return on the voyage by judicious

purchases of West Indian sugar. Profits varied enormously
and unpredictably. A ship that successfully completed the
round journey might show a profit of over 100 per cent
upon all outlays of the voyage; but other ships might fail
to purchase a full cargo of slaves, or be lost completely by
shipwreck, slave mutiny, or enemy action in wartime. In
addition to these hazards, there was some tendency for the
'terms of trade' to deteriorate during the eighteenth century; buying prices rose as competition increased and
African slave-dealers learned to bargain more keenly, and
it was not always possible to pass on the whole increase to
the planters. (Against this, costs could be reduced by
building larger ships, reducing deaths at sea, or cutting
down the emoluments of officers and crew.) Slaving remained a risky business, and those without the capital to
bear occasional heavy losses might well go under. Hence,
in the early days of private trade, the expenses of a voyage
were often spread among several partners; hence too the
later tendency for Liverpool's trade to be dominated by
fewer but larger traders.

Still, many private traders — freed from the obligation
to contribute directly to the overhead expenses represented
by the forts — did prosper. The civic history of Liverpool
during the eighteenth century can provide many examples
of this. Some at least of these profits were re-invested in the
growing new industries of the hinterland. Families like the
Heywoods, who engaged in the Liverpool slave-trade
(though not as their major activity), also operated in
insurance, as bankers in Manchester, as cloth manufacturers in Wakefield. But the contribution of slave-trade
capital to the industrial growth of the later eighteenth
century is impossible to measure quantitatively, and cor-
respondingly easy to exaggerate.

One argument used to show that the slave-trade was

especially advantageous to the nation emphasized its
stimulus to British shipping, which must prosper in peace-
time if the Navy was to be capable of expansion in war.
Up to a point, this argument had force. Since slaving involved lengthy ocean voyages, it did employ a greater
proportion of the nation's shipping than the value of goods
carried would suggest. Moreover, it encouraged the building of relatively big ships, up to 500 tons or more; and,
since it was necessary to guard and attend to a human
cargo, these usually carried a relatively large crew, with a
good proportion of nautical tradesmen, such as coopers,
armourers, and cooks. So when the trade came under
humanitarian criticism, national heroes like Admiral Rod-
ney warmly defended it as an essential 'nursery of seamen'.
But though the trade certainly stimulated the growth of
British shipping, and of ancillary industries, it did so in a
way that was wasteful as well as inhumane. Clarkson and
the Abolitionists had no difficulty in demonstrating that
mortality among seamen in slavers was substantially
greater than in any other oceanic trade. This was a nursery of seamen with a terribly high death-rate. In the early
stages of British maritime growth it may have had a stimulating effect; but once there was a chance of alternative
trades being captured by British shipping, it was folly to
talk of giving this one any preferential treatment.

Still, the slave-trade seemed to measure up well to acknowledged principles of economic orthodoxy, and only
when those principles became subject to fundamental criticism was opposition manifested by more than a few isolated
intellectuals or religious men. For most of the century,
slaving was not merely an acceptable activity, but a
thoroughly respectable one. Even those who actually
manned the slave ships were not all base-born and brutal
ruffians; though some had all these qualities, others were

honest Christian men who saw no problem in justifying their business activities, or no need to try. And the merchants who sent them formed part of a growing commercial class which inter-married, and co-operated in business and politics, with landed families up to the highest in the land. Property founded on slave-dealing, like property founded on West Indian slavery, formed part of the wealth of a powerful but amorphous ruling class, not yet deeply divided by social or political antagonisms; the strength of the slaving interest lay in this community of interest more than in its own calculable wealth. Only gradually did men begin to ask whether different forms of economic relationship, paying more respect to human dignity, might not prove equally or more advantageous to the wealth of the nation.

Attempts to justify the trade must rest chiefly on its role in the development of the American tropics. In modern jargon, the trade might be defended as a method of organizing large-scale migration of labour in order to stimulate economic growth. The strong arms of the Africans, contemporary apologists argued, would be employed far more productively in America than in Africa (some went on to claim that their standards of consumption, and even their 'Liberty and Happiness', were improved by the move). But even if human beings can be treated as a 'commodity' like any other — a view objectionable on many grounds — eighteenth-century plantation slavery remains vulnerable to purely economic criticism.

The first objection is based on the extremely low rate of human reproduction in most slave colonies. This is partly because the number of births was relatively small. Only about one-third of the slaves landed in the West Indies by the Royal African Company, for example, were females; their fertility rate was not high. and many infants died.

The death-rate was also high — partly because of physio-
logical or psychological disorders induced by forcible
migration, partly because of cruelty or overwork. So long
as slaves could be bought cheaply, planters had little economic inducement to conserve life; thus colonies which had
once acquired sufficient slaves to develop all their lands still
went on importing replacements. During the eighteenth
century, however, there is evidence of some improvement.
The cost of new slaves, rising during the century from £20
or less to £50 or more for an active male; the fear, latterly,
that new imports might be prohibited by law; possibly
even a more humane and enlightened view of self-in-
terests — these things together caused some West Indians
at least to pay more attention to feeding, hygiene, and
general conditions of labour, to try to buy more females,
and to improve the rudimentary facilities for childbirth.
Some plantations, like John Pinney's in Nevis, were maintaining their labour force by natural increase from about
1775; by the nineteenth century, natural increase was the
chief source of the rapid growth of the slave population of
the United States.

But even if waste could be reduced, in the sense that
more productive labour was obtained for each slave im-
ported, the availability of plentiful supplies of cheap labour
might still impede economic growth by discouraging planters from investing more capital in their estates. Sugar-
growers who had plenty of slaves for the arduous but
unskilled task of planting canes were slow to consider
introducing even so simple a development as the plough.
Capital sunk in slaves could offer just as serious an obstacle
to technical experiment and progress as capital sunk in
obsolescent machinery.

Less directly, there were economic implications in the
tensions of plantation society. Fear of insurrection was.

D2

never far below the surface in communities stratified along racial lines; it expressed itself in the disciplinary excesses of the more notoriously brutal planters. Between the slave proletariat (a huge majority in most West Indian islands, a minority of up to 40 per cent in the American South), and the white settlers, themselves of very varied social status, there was a generally discontented middle group of 'free people of colour', mulattoes and manumitted slaves who were often suspected of subversive aims. Slave societies could rarely feel secure; though apprehensions for the future varied greatly in intensity according to time and place, they inevitably tended to inhibit economic growth.

But it was in Africa itself that the Atlantic slave-trade was most harmful. Its most obvious consequence was depopulation. An estimate of 70,000 or more for the number of slaves landed annually in America by the 1780s has already been quoted; to this must be added 10 per cent or more for losses at sea. Then there were those who died in Africa. In the seventeenth century the Royal African Company seems to have found that about 10 per cent of its slaves bought on the Gold Coast died in the forts while awaiting embarkation. Others would die in African hands while being marched to the coast, and many more would be killed in internal wars and raids, sometimes undertaken with the aim of obtaining saleable prisoners. At a rough approximation, it would seem that as many as fifteen million slaves in all may have been landed in America, and that possibly as many persons again died in Africa or at sea. Something like half of these losses occurred during the eighteenth century. Although some slave-exporting areas, like the Niger delta, may have been over-populated, Africa as a whole was not; hence, even leaving moral judgments aside, this was a grievous loss to the continent.

There would nevertheless have been compensations if

the trade had acted as a stimulus to economic growth within Africa. And contemporaries did indeed talk smugly about extending 'the blessings of civilisation' to that continent, encouraged by observing in some coastal areas the small class of African entrepreneurs, enriched by the slave-trade, who were acquiring European skills and a smattering of European culture. Some Africans were baptized by the occasional priest who accompanied the slavers; a few sent their children to school in Europe; others learned crafts within the European settlements. But the new wealth and new skills were rarely put to productive use, as can be inferred from study of the list of goods sent to Africa in exchange for slaves. Alcoholic liquors, contrary to legend, account for a relatively small proportion; gunpowder, though no more important financially, had a special importance as giving power to its possessors; by far the biggest items were textiles, hardware and beads — harmless and useful consumption goods, but contributing little to economic life, and in some cases actually replacing traditional articles of local manufacture. Any productive tool more significant than a machete is absent from the list. Apart from the introduction of some important new food-crops, a development not integrally connected with the slave-trade as such, Africa gained few material objects of lasting importance in return for these formidable exports of men.

During the eighteenth century there was repeatedly talk in Europe about developing new economic relationships with Africa. Some hoped to find extended markets by pressing 'a friendly, humane and civilized commerce' into the interior; others talked of encouraging new forms of production, notably plantation crops like cotton, sugar, and indigo. One of the reasons why such projects came to nothing exposes the folly of the view that the slave-trade could civilize Africa; slaving and commercial agriculture, it gradually became clear, were competitive activities. Quite apart from the insecurity and waste in areas where slaves were obtained by fighting, wherever there was a keen demand for slaves at the coast it would be found more profitable to export surplus labour than to employ it for speculative agricultural schemes. African entrepreneurs with interests in the established system were more interested in obstructing such experiments as were tried.

This is not to say that they would all have succeeded. There were many natural difficulties in the way of commercial penetration of the interior, or of a spectacular increase in African production of foodstuffs or industrial raw materials. But the first condition of progress in either direction was to control the slave-trade. This trade was already so well entrenched, in African as well as in European society, that armed force would be needed to destroy it — naval action in the Atlantic, and eventually military operations inland. By the end of the eighteenth century some Europeans, envisaging Africa's future as a producing area within a world economy rather than as a reservoir of labour for the plantations, were ready to pay at least part of this price. But shipments across the Atlantic continued until the 1860s, and only in the present century was organized slave traffic within West Africa suppressed.

BIBLIOGRAPHICAL NOTE

There is a great deal of information about the later years of the slave-trade in the reports of the various committees of enquiry appointed at the instigation of the Abolitionists. The most important of these may be found in *Accounts and Papers* (1789), Vols. XXV and XXVI. Elizabeth Donann's *Documents Illustrative of the History of the Slave Trade to America* (4 vols.,

Washington, D.C., 1930–5) is a useful compilation of primary material. The accounts of the slave-traders themselves often repay reading; the authors of some are named in the text. Thomas Clarkson's *History . . . of the Abolition of the African Slave-Trade* (2 vols., London, 1808) is also informative, though the author's purpose in writing must be remembered.

K. G. Davies's *The Royal African Company* (London, 1957) is extremely valuable. For the later organization of the British trade, see E. C. Martin, *The British West African Settlements, 1750–1821* (London, 1927): and an article by F. E. Hyde and others on 'The Nature and Profitability of the Liverpool Slave Trade' in *Economic History Review* (2nd series, V, 1953). Eric Williams, *Capitalism and Slavery* (Chapel Hill, 1944), takes another approach. On the French slave-trade, see Gaston Martin, *Nantes au XVIIIᵉ siècle; l'ère des Négriers* (Paris, 1931), and his *Histoire de l'Esclavage dans les Colonies françaises* (Paris, 1948). For a short discussion of effects on Africa, J. D. Fage, *An Introduction to the History of West Africa* (Cambridge, 1955); for the West Indies, J. H. Parry and P. M. Sherlock, *A Short History of the West Indies* (London, 1956). See also H. A. Wyndham, *The Atlantic and Slavery* (London, 1935).

Figures relating to the Royal African Company are taken from Davies's book, as is also my quotation from John Snow. My statements about British foreign trade in the later eighteenth century are based on the following totals for the years 1784–90, which I derive from D. Macpherson, *Annals of Commerce*, Vol. IV (London, 1805).

British imports from Africa -	£667,569
British exports to Africa - -	£5,061,914
of which British manufactures were - -	£3,350,496
British exports to B.W.I. - -	£10,564,895
Total British exports, 1784–90 -	£121,322,655

VI

Customs and Manners

by JAMES LAVER

THE 'catastrophic' theory once dear to biologists has now been generally abandoned by historians also. History knows no clean cuts; it is a perpetual state of transition, and even the convenient division of Time into centuries is frequently misleading. When did the eighteenth century begin and when did it end? It would be possible to maintain that it began with the flight of James II and the accession of a Constitutional Monarch, and ended with the French Revolution — or with the Battle of Waterloo.

Yet, in the perspective of Time, the eighteenth century does seem to have a kind of unity, even if the subjects of Queen Anne would have found many things to surprise them in the England of George III. For the greater part of the century men wore the same kind of clothes, the same three-cornered hat; they even persisted in the astounding practice of shaving off their own hair and wearing wigs. Even women, although their fashions changed sufficiently in the first two decades to astonish Addison, retained a certain family look. We are in no danger of confusing them with Elizabethans or Victorians. Headdresses may rise and fall, skirts expand or shrink again, but the eighteenth-century lady presents a fairly consistent and unblurred image to the mind.

It is the same with society itself. England throughout the century, in spite of expanding trade and the beginnings of industrialism, remained based upon a rural economy. Wealth was still firmly rooted in the land, with the typically English division into landed proprietor, tenant farmer, and farm labourer. It was not really until the end of the century, when the 'Nabobs' began to bring in the spoils of India, that the balance was disturbed. The typical English figure is John Bull, not a peasant like the typical figures of other countries, but a country gentleman in a hunting coat. He presided over the typical English village; its inhabitants were his tenants or his servants, and the parson was frequently his younger brother. No doubt there were many Tony Lumpkins to set against one Sir Roger de Coverley, but the pattern was the same.

The aristocracy itself was not very dissimilar. In England there was no Versailles to draw the nobles to the Court of an almost absolute monarch. The great landed proprietors, like their humbler brethren, spent much of their time on their country estates. They were not courtiers, but local kings. They regarded the attractions of London with suspicion, and if, like Mr Hardcastle, they occasionally allowed their women-folk to come up 'to Town, to rub off the rust a little', they too feared that the result would only be to bring back vanity and affectation.

We tend to think of the eighteenth century as an age of elegance and polite manners; if we could return we would probably be astonished at its coarseness and insensitivity. Even fine ladies used strong language and drank 'strong waters', and boorish drunkenness was often to be found among 'fine gentlemen'. In the earlier years of the century at least there was more refinement in the middle classes, especially if they had come under the influence of the Dissenting Academies.

Much credit for teaching the aristocracy manners must be given to Richard Nash. This remarkable man was himself of humble origin, and his means of livelihood were somewhat dubious. He was, in short, a professional gambler; but he was a man of excellent address and a real talent for organization. Queen Anne's visit to Bath in 1703 had made the place fashionable, but the amenities offered were still primitive in the extreme. Dancing took place on the bowling green, for there was, as yet, no Assembly Room; card parties and the like were held in a tent. Dress was informal, the men wearing top-boots and swords, the ladies aprons.

Beau Nash, as he was called, set himself to reform all this. He provided an Assembly Room, hired a good orchestra, raised a large sum of money by subscription for improving the roads in the vicinity and, most important of all, drew up a series of rules, which he posted up in the Pump Room. He forbade swords and duelling, smoking and slovenly dress, and he was, by sheer force of personality, able to impose his will. When the Duchess of Queensberry defied him by appearing in an apron, he insisted, with infinite respect, on removing it with his own hands and, throwing it among the waiting women, declared that aprons were only fit for abigails.

In a few years he was recognized as King of Bath, and Bath itself as an aristocratic school of manners. Henceforward there was a progressive improvement in the habits of polite society, so much so that we tend to think of the eighteenth century as a period of formality and decorum, at least on the surface. Sometimes this decorum was pushed to extreme lengths; so much so, that Lord Chesterfield in 1751 was advising his son to 'learn to sit genteelly in different companies, to loll genteelly, and with good manners, in those companies where you are authorised to be free: and to sit up respectfully where the same freedom is not allowable. . . . Take particular care that the motions

of your hands and arms be free and graceful, for the gen-
teelness of a man consists more in them than in anything
else.'

Another civilizing influence on the upper classes was the
Grand Tour. By the middle of the century it had become
an established custom for the aristocracy to send their sons
abroad. 'Where one Englishman travelled in the reigns of
the first two Georges, ten now go on a grand tour. Indeed
to such a pitch has the spirit of travelling come in the kingdom, that there is scarce a citizen of large fortune but takes
a flying view of France, Italy and Germany in a summer's
excursion.'[1]

Dean Tucker, in his *Instructions for Travellers*, published
in 1757, sets forth the motives which inspired these ex-
peditions:

First, to make curious Collections, as Natural Philosophers,
Virtuosos, or Antiquarians. *Secondly*, to improve in Painting,
Architecture and Music. *Thirdly*, to obtain the reputation of
being Men of Vertu, and of an elegant Taste. *Fourthly*, to
acquire foreign Airs, and adorn their dear Persons with fine
Cloaths and new Fashions, and their Conversations with new
Phrases. Or *Fifthly*, to rub off local Prejudices (which is in-
deed the most commendable Motive though not the most
prevailing) and to acquire that impartial view of Men and
Things, which no one single country can afford.

Although for many young blades the Grand Tour must
have been little more than an opportunity for dissipation,
there is no doubt that a proportion of them at least did
acquire a more elegant taste, especially in architecture
and painting, as the collections in the splendid houses
surviving from the eighteenth century still bear witness.

In London, among the most potent civilizing influences
must be reckoned the coffee-house. The first had been

[1] *Letters concerning the present State of England*, 1772.

opened under the Commonwealth, and, by the beginning of the eighteenth century, there were nearly three thousand in the metropolis alone. They were already specialized in their clientele, the merchants frequenting Garraway's, Jonathan's, Tom's and Lloyd's near the Royal Exchange. The booksellers met at the Chapter off Paternoster Row, and the physicians at Button's in Cornhill. The wits gathered in the coffee-houses of Covent Garden, and the men of fashion in those of St James's Street and Pall Mall.

These last developed, as by a natural evolution, into clubs, originally gambling clubs, and some of them (although they have given up gambling) still survive, under the names of their original proprietors: e.g. Boodle's and White's. In the City there was a somewhat different development. Lloyd's, which already, in Addison's time, was a meeting place for merchants interested in shipping and foreign trade, became in time the world-famous institution which still bears the same name. Jonathan's and Garraway's provided the starting point for the Stock Exchange. But it is with the civilizing influence of the literary coffee-houses that we are here concerned.

'The coffee-house', says M. Dorothy George,[1] 'was a godsend especially to the young man who came to town, as Johnson did, to earn a living from the booksellers. It mitigated the squalor of Grub Street, offered a chance of introduction to the wits, and provided the necessary good address; as Johnson was told before he came to London, "a man might live in a garret for eighteen pence a week; few people would enquire where he lodged, and if they did, it was easy to say, 'Sir, I am to be found at such a place'." By spending threepence in a coffee-house he might be for some hours every day in very good company.'

[1] 'London and the Life of the Town', in *Johnson's England*, edited by A. S. Turberville, London, 1933.

One of the attractions of the coffee-house was the possibility of reading the newspapers, but at the Bedford Head, 'under the piazza' of Covent Garden, politics were 'seldom brought upon the carpet'.[1] It was, however, 'every night crowded with men of parts. Almost everyone you meet is a polite scholar and a wit, jokes and *bon mots* are echoed from box to box; every branch of literature is critically examined, and the merit of every production of the theatres, weighed and determined.' The modern budding author cannot but regret that no such institution is available to him today.

Neither the fine taste of the dilettanti nor the literary interests of the London wits, however, had much immediate effect on the lower classes, or even on the humbler landed gentry. The typical squire maintained his prejudices against all things foreign, and if he and his fellows did not, like Goering, reach for a revolver at the mere mention of the word Culture, they were at least likely to reach for a riding-whip. Says A. E. Richardson:[2]

As a class, they were hardly remarkable for refinement or polished manners. The average squire visited London only if he held a seat in Parliament. His conversation was of agriculture, horses and livestock with, of course, the eternal topic of hunting. After administering justice to poachers and others in the Hall, he would inspect his stables and kennels, dealing out praise or abuse to his ostlers, grooms and keepers. Groups of the gentry would arrange weekly dinners at which they feasted heavily, drank more than copiously, and discussed the usual topics with a spice of politics. . . . While every squire possessed a library, the books were seldom consulted beyond their titles, for intellectual recreations were apt to pall before the pleasures of a hard day out of doors

[1] *Memoirs of the Bedford Head Coffee-House*, 1763.
[2] *Georgian England. A Survey of Social Life, Trades, Industries and Art from 1700 to 1820*, London, 1931.

and somnolent relaxation before a great wood fire in the
evenings.

The rural communities were almost self-sufficing. The
very tools of agriculture were made locally, and the produce of the land sufficed for all requirements. It has been
estimated that, with the exception of sugar, the import
trade of England in the first half of the eighteenth century
was entirely in articles of luxury or semi-luxury, and these
were naturally absorbed for the most part by London and
other towns. The village was to all intents and purposes a
self-contained unit, and few of its inhabitants ventured
more than a few miles from its borders.

This was partly due, of course, to the difficulties of transport. For some years after the Restoration there were only
six stage coaches in the whole of England, and things were
not much better in the reign of Queen Anne. It was thought
wonderful when the journey from London to Oxford was
accomplished in a single day. Even as late as 1742 the
ordinary stage coach which left London for Oxford at
7 a.m. did not arrive at High Wycombe until 5 p.m., and
stayed there for the night. The journey from London to
York took six days.

It was not merely a matter of proceeding slowly; the
roughness of the roads was such that bumps and jolts were
inevitable, especially when riding in vehicles without
springs. Coaches were frequently upset, not because they
were travelling too fast, but because the ruts in the roads
were as deep as trenches in dry weather, and positive
quagmires in wet. Added to all this was the real danger of
being stopped by highwaymen. Even if this has been exaggerated by romantic writers, readers of Vanbrugh's *Journey
to London*, written in 1699, will remember that the arma-
ment provided for the party included 'the family basket-

hilt sword, the great Turkish scimitar, the old blunderbuss, a good bag of bullets, and a great horn of gunpowder'. It is small wonder that most people, even if they could afford the expense of a journey, preferred to stay at home.

Things gradually improved. In 1754 a new vehicle, 'The Flying Coach', was advertised in the following terms: 'However incredible it may appear, this coach will actually (barring accidents) arrive in London in four days and a half after leaving Manchester.' In 1757 a rival coach, a 'flying machine on steel springs', travelled from Liverpool to London in three days. Yet in 1760 it still took four days for a coach carrying six passengers inside to reach the capital from Exeter. A few years later the time had been shortened to two days, but it was not until 1784 that the journey was first accomplished in thirty-two hours. This was only made possible by the improvement in road-surfaces associated with the name of John Macadam.

There were not lacking those who lamented these changes. We find even the enlightened Arthur Young, in his *Annals of Agriculture*, published in 1789, remarking that the flocking of yokels to London '*was* no easy matter, when a stage-coach was four or five days creeping an hundred miles . . . *But now!* a country fellow one hundred miles from London, jumps on a stage-coach in the morning, and for eight or ten shillings gets to London by night.' If Daniel Defoe, who brought out his *Tour Through the Whole Island of Great Britain* between 1724 and 1727, could have returned to the scene of his travels sixty or seventy years later, he would have been astonished at the revolution which had taken place.

Notwithstanding the extreme primitiveness of life for the greater part of the population there was very little social discontent. The eighteenth-century Englishman, of all classes, was a sturdy creature, and if he could find a roof for his head, eat enough beef and drink enough beer, he seems to have been contented with his lot. Paradoxically, in an age of rigid class distinctions, there was less snobbery than in later ages, when the distinctions between the classes were more blurred. Even the fine lady was on more intimate terms with her social inferiors than her counterpart a hundred years later. The daughters of the great house took a hand in the still-room and even in the dairy; the notion that a 'lady' must do nothing useful without losing caste had not yet emerged. It was beginning to do so towards the end of the century, when we find a sudden increase in what might be called 'parlour-crafts': watercolour painting, embroidery, paper-cutting, and the like.

The gentleman also, if he lived in the country, was on familiar terms with his grooms and keepers, and found a common interest with them in sport, although it must be confessed that many of the 'sports' popular at the time were brutal and barbarous to an extreme degree.

Cock-fighting had been practised since the Middle Ages at least, and had often received royal patronage. Henry VIII built a cockpit at Whitehall; there were several others in London, and many elsewhere. The birds, clipped of their combs and provided with steel spurs, were matched against one another in pairs, or in a 'battle royal' in which a number of birds were left to fight among themselves until only one survived. The attraction, apart from the excitement of the spectacle, was, of course, gambling, and the stakes were high. An engraving by Hogarth shows exactly what the interior of a cockpit was like: it had a kind of raised circular table in the middle, round which the spectators stood. All classes are represented among them, from the fine gentleman who seems to be taking the bets, to draymen, carters and the like, all drawn together by the prevailing passion.

Equally brutal and even less 'sporting' was the practice of cock-throwing, in which short staves were thrown at cocks in order to kill them or break their legs. The word 'cock-shy' still survives as a relic of this amusement. Sometimes the unfortunate cock was confined in a special earthenware vessel which allowed the head and the tail to protrude. The object was to break the vessel by throwing at it, and when this was accomplished the successful player claimed the cock. Goose-riding was a rural sport. A goose with its neck well greased was hung up by its legs from the bough of a tree. The competitors rode underneath it and tried to *pull off its head* as they passed.

We hear less of bear-baiting than in Elizabethan times, when, as we know, it was sufficiently popular to rival the attractions of Shakespeare's Globe. Bull-baiting continued in the eighteenth century all over England. Villages and small towns were visited by the bullward, or bullard, who led his beast from place to place, tied him to a stake in the ground, and invited the bull-hankers or fanciers to set their dogs on him for a shilling.

Bull-running was also practised. A bull was purchased by subscription and let loose in the street, shop-doors and gates being carefully closed beforehand. The bull was then chased with bull-clubs, the only concession to humanity being the proviso that such clubs should not have 'any iron upon them'. Badger-baiting was even more disgusting, a chain being passed *through* the animal's tail and dogs set on him. The badger usually put up a good fight, and might kill several dogs before he was dispatched.

Public opinion has long since condemned all such 'sports'. Hunting — of stag, fox, and hare — is still with us, although even this has begun to be questioned in modern times. It was extremely popular in the eighteenth century, but was less well organized and certainly less ritualistic than it is today. A special costume for fox-hunting was not yet *de rigueur*, and most followers of the hounds simply wore the country dress of the period.

Hunting was, indeed, the principal occupation of the rural squire, and the local parson was not above joining in the chase. Some 'squarsons' even wore their riding boots in the pulpit, so as to waste as little time as possible in changing their clothes. It was even possible for the London tradesman to join in, for there were recognized hunts in Epping Forest, at Muswell Hill, and at Enfield. It is a reminder of how near London then was to the open fields to learn that it was the custom for the chief porter at the Middle Temple to blow a horn 'to recall the young gentlemen to their studies from rabbit coursing on Lambeth marshes'. Devotees of shooting were under the disadvantage of having no adequate fowling piece, the old flint-lock still being in general use, but the sporting prints of the end of the century show that by that time it was popular enough.

Horse-racing drew great crowds, but special race-courses were few, and contests were generally held on commons or any piece of open ground. The horses were bred rather for staying power than for speed. The standard of riding was low, jostling and crossing were common occurrences, and jockeys were known to use their whips against their rivals. None the less, towards the end of the period we are considering, most of the classic races had been established: the St Leger in 1776, the Oaks in 1779, the Derby in 1780.

Football, although popular on Shrove Tuesday and Ash Wednesday, bore very little relation to any of the varieties of the modern game. It still followed the medieval custom of playing in the street and allowing anybody to join in. In narrow streets like those of the City of London it could be a danger not only to the players but to anyone passing by. The goals might be anywhere (in Ashbourne, for example, they were three miles apart) and it was permissible to handle the ball. In fact, there were no rules whatever. Casualties were frequent, and Friendly Societies excluded those hurt at football from all benefit payments.

Cricket was not quite in the same state of chaos. We hear as early as 1705 that 'A Cricket match will be plaid between eleven gentlemen of the west part of Kent and those of Chatham for eleven guineas a man.' This meant that about £120 — a considerable sum in those days — changed hands as a result of the match. County cricket may be said to have been established by the middle of the century, and it was in 1750 that the famous Hambledon Club was founded, with regular grounds to play on. But it was not until 1774 that definite rules were first laid down, limiting, for instance, the size of the bat. By the close of the century three stumps had taken the place of two.

An attempt to regulate boxing was made by Jack Broughton, who became Champion of England in 1740; indeed 'Broughton's Rules' continued in operation until they were succeeded by the 'Queensberry Rules' of the nineteenth century. Broughton introduced 'mufflers' or, as we should say, boxing gloves for practice, but the actual fights were conducted with bare fists. It has been suggested that bare-fist fighting, although more spectacularly brutal — or more obviously bloody — than glove-fighting, was, in fact, less dangerous, as the hands protected by gloves are able to deliver a harder blow. The fact that the solar plexus punch had not yet been discovered explains the curious stance of eighteenth-century boxers as shown in contemporary sporting prints. The ropes surrounding the ring were originally provided to keep out the spectators who were only too likely to join in the fight, and the raising of the floor had the same object.

Even in London, life was lived to an astonishing degree out of doors. Nowadays we tend to think that it is the foreigner who sits on café seats or in beer-gardens, and we forget that foreigners in the eighteenth century regarded the pleasure-garden as an English invention. The French even called their own imitation 'Wauxhall'.

The original Vauxhall was situated on the south bank of the river, near the modern Vauxhall Bridge; its rival, Ranelagh, was at Chelsea. Vauxhall was larger and more popular, but the *beau monde* did not despise it, and one of its attractions for humbler folk was the chance of gazing upon 'the great', with their stars and garters and embroidered coats. Concerts were given, and quite elaborate meals were provided (the patrons of Ranelagh had to content themselves, except on gala nights, with tea and bread and butter), and as a mid-century chronicler[1] remarks: 'After the music is ended for the night, 'tis vastly agreable to wander round the ranges of pavilions, and gaze at the numberless parties (some of whom are frequently attended by French horns) supping in their several bowers. . . . Many have wondered how it could be possible for three or four hundred persons to be regularly entertained at different tables at one and the same time.' We have the word of James Boswell that it was a place of 'elegant and innocent entertainment . . . particularly adapted to the taste of the English nation, there being a mixture of curious shew — gay exhibition — musick, vocal and instrumental, not too refined for the general ear; for all of which only a shilling is paid: and though last not least — good eating and drinking for those who choose to purchase that regale.'

Ranelagh was quieter and more refined, the music being listened to more seriously. The chief attraction was the

[1] Anon., *A Sketch of the Spring Gardens at Vauxhall*, c. 1750.

great Rotunda, which impressed Samuel Johnson, and of which several drawings and engravings have come down to us. Both gardens were attractively illuminated. They opened in the spring and closed at the end of August.

These two, however, were not the only pleasure-gardens in London; in fact the town was surrounded by a ring of them of varying degrees of social *ton*. Most of them were situated to the north, in St Pancras, Islington, and Kentish Town, all, at that period, rural or semi-rural. Here were Baggnigge Wells, Sadler's Wells, and Islington Spa, all frequented by the 'middle and lower ranks', although the Islington establishment was once visited by Princess Amelia, who came to 'drink the waters'. Concerts and balls were given, and even on Sundays the gardens were much frequented for tea-drinking. Games such as skittles and trap-and-ball were played, and Islington even had a cricket pitch.

All this seems harmless enough, but south of the river there were gardens, such as the Dog and Duck, of a rather different character, where highwaymen and loose women gathered. The *Public Advertiser* was complaining in 1775 that, 'of the many thousands that resort to such places, very few can support the expense, which brings many of the men to the gallows and the women upon the town'. Still, many respectable citizens seem to have used the tea-gardens and the taverns round London for Sunday outings, and it is plain that the Sabbath gloom so much remarked upon by foreigners a century later was no part of English life in the eighteenth century.

The accessibility of pleasure-resorts at this period reminds us that even London was still a comparatively small town. The country was quite near. The new squares at Bloomsbury, sometimes, like Queen Anne's Square, left open to the north, afforded a vista of open fields and, beyond, the hills of Hampstead and Highgate. Tottenham Court Road, except at its southern end, ran through open fields. Wigmore Street, then called Wigmore Row, had houses only on the south side. To the west lay Hyde Park, not yet surrounded by bricks and mortar. There was a marsh beyond Buckingham House, and Chelsea was a village. Even the Londoner was in touch with rural life, and of course this connection was even more noticeable in provincial towns.

We are so accustomed to think of towns as vast agglomerations that we need to be reminded that Bristol, in the eighteenth century the second largest town in England, had no more than 100,000 inhabitants. Manchester, although growing rapidly, had, in 1769, only 30,000, Liverpool 40,000, Birmingham 30,000, and Leeds 17,000. Wesley, in his *Journal*, speaks of the 'street' of Northampton. There were indeed no more than 5,000 people living there at the time of his visit.

In places of such size problems of crowding, sanitation and water supply had hardly yet arisen. Foreign visitors frequently remark on the cleanliness of English people. A Frenchman noted in 1726 that 'not a week passes by but well-kept houses are washed twice in the seven days and that from top to bottom; and even every morning most kitchens, staircases and entrances are scrubbed. . . . English women and men are very clean: not a day passes by without their washing their hands, arms, faces, necks and throats in cold water, and that in winter as well as in summer.'[1] We hear, however, nothing about baths.

In the slums of London things were very different. As late as 1760 every householder was responsible for removing the dirt and mending the pavement outside his own

[1] C. de Saussure; *A Foreign View of England in the Reigns of George I and George II*, translated and edited by Madame van Muyden, London, 1902.

dwelling. As he very rarely did either the state of the streets may be readily imagined. Rubbish accumulated, 'slops' were simply emptied out of the upper windows, dead cats lay in the gutter. In wet weather it was impossible to cross the streets without being splashed with mud. Hogarth's engravings provide a vivid picture of these conditions.

However, if we consider the period between Samuel Johnson's arrival in London in 1737 and his death in 1784, we shall be compelled to register many improvements. Various Paving Bills were presented to Parliament without success, and we find Johnson himself complaining in 1741 that:

> the present neglect of cleansing and paving the streets is such as ought not to be borne, that the passenger is every where either surprised or endangered by neglected chasms, or offended and obstructed by mountains of filth, is well known to every one that has passed a single day in this great city; and that this grievance is without remedy, is a sufficient proof, that no magistrate has at present power to remove it.

The magistrates of Westminster acted in 1762, and those of the City four years later. The removal of refuse and the paving of the streets were made a public responsibility. Raised sidewalks were built and the cobbles of the streets replaced by flat stones. Projecting shop signs, which had often proved a danger and an annoyance to the public, especially in a high wind, when they creaked abominably, were replaced by signs affixed to the walls.

The result of these measures was a great improvement in public health and a consequent increase in population. The number of births did not increase, but not quite so many children died, though infant mortality was still shocking by modern standards. Mrs Thrale, for example, succeeded in raising only four out of her family of eleven, and the graveyards of the period are full of pathetic memorials. It is estimated that in the first sixty years of the century the population of England and Wales increased by 23 per cent, and in the remaining forty years by 32 per cent.

This was only made possible by improvement in agriculture and, towards the end of the century, by the growth of manufactures. This is not the place to enlarge upon the work of men like Coke of Norfolk; it is sufficient to note that the production of root crops made it possible to keep cattle through the winter, with the result that fresh meat took the place of salt meat and that more milk was available. It is thought also that the marked improvement in public health between the reign of Queen Anne and that of George III was partly due to the substitution of glass drinking vessels for the old uncleanable leather ones, and of earthenware or china plates for wooden and pewter platters. The decrease in gin-drinking among the lower classes, brought about by more stringent regulations halfway through the century, may also have had something to do with it.

So much for the physical health of the community. What of its mental and spiritual health? The eighteenth century is not usually considered a religious period in English history. Most of the theological controversies of the previous century seemed to have faded into a general tolerant indifference. The Government deliberately chose bishops for their Erastian or Latitudinarian views, and this attitude was reflected in the general life of the Church. Dissenters and Roman Catholics were, of course, excluded from all public offices, but this did not prevent the former at least from exercising considerable influence, especially among the rising middle classes.

The lower classes, however, especially in the mining districts and the growing industrial centres, were almost

entirely unprovided for; and it was this state of affairs that
John Wesley and those who sympathised with him set out
to remedy. He had to face much opposition from those
who feared the extravagances of enthusiasm (it is typical
of the eighteenth century that 'enthusiasm' was used as a
term of abuse even by Wesley himself) and preferred the
calm of the Established Church to be undisturbed. By his
tireless exertions and great organizing capacity, Wesley
and his followers did succeed in reaching many who were
outside the scope of the ordinary parish ministrations, and
it has been claimed, not without reason, that, by con-
fining discontent and reforming zeal to religious channels,
he did much to avert an English equivalent of the French
Revolution.

There can be little doubt that the final quarter of the
century witnessed a general increase in sensibility. In social
matters this showed itself in prison reform, and in the
beginnings of agitation for the abolition of the slave trade.
In art and literature we call it the Romantic Movement.
There was a new feeling for the beauties of nature, and a
feeling for the past, which was sometimes pushed to extravagant lengths, as in the early 'Gothick' revival. In
education Rousseau's cult of the noble savage resulted at
least in a new attitude to the child. It is not without significance that, from about 1770 onwards, children began
to be provided with a dress in which they could play in
comfort, instead of being expected to resemble miniature
adults, with ruffles, dressed hair and a sword, or, in the
case of girls, with tight corsets and hoops. Tender hearts
became almost fashionable; it was no longer considered a
disgrace to be a 'Man of Feeling'.

In the final decade of the eighteenth century we can
already see the shape of things to come in the nineteenth.
The wig and the embroidered coat had given place to a

man's own hair and a coat of plain cloth. The top-hat was already beginning to replace the tricorne which had lasted so long. Women had thrown away their hoops and were adopting what they fondly imagined to be the clothes of Ancient Greece. England, from a little country on the outside edge of Europe, had become the centre of a great Empire. The Industrial Revolution was under way. Many seeds had been planted which were to come to fruition a generation later. We cannot share the contempt of the Victorians for a period in which so much was accomplished, and when the image of the free-born Englishman impressed itself on the rest of the world as worthy of respect and imitation.

SUGGESTIONS FOR FURTHER READING

Strutt, J., *Sports and Pastimes of the People of England*, 1801.

Sydney, W. C., *England and the English in the Eighteenth Century*, Ward & Downey, 1892.

Wroth, W. W. and E. A., *London Pleasure Gardens of the Eighteenth Century*, Macmillan, 1896.

Saussure, C. de, *A Foreign View of England in the Reigns of George I and George II*, translated by Madame van Muyden, Murray, 1902.

Chancellor, H. B., *The Eighteenth Century in London*, Batsford, 1920.

Woodforde, J., *The Diary of a Country Parson*, edited by John Beresford, Oxford University Press, 1926–31.

Turberville, A. S., *English Men and Manners in the Eighteenth Century*, Oxford University Press, 1926.

—— *Johnson's England*, Clarendon Press, 1933.

Defoe, D., *Tour through the Whole Island of Great Britain, 1724–7*, Everyman, 1928.

Young, A., *Tour through the Southern Counties, 1768*, London, 1772.

Young, A., *Tour through the North of England, 1770*, London, 1770.

Richardson, A. E., *Georgian England*, Batsford, 1931.

Wesley, J., *Journal*, Oliphants, 1952.

Willett Cunnington, C., and Cunnington, P., *Handbook of English Costume in the Eighteenth Century*, Faber, 1957.

VII

The Grand Tour

by R. J. WHITE

SIR,
I understand you have left Eton, and probably intend to go to one of those Schools of Vice, the Universities. If, however, you chuse to travel, I will give you £500 per annum. . . .

THOMAS COKE, of Longford Hall in Derbyshire, remembered to the end of his very long life[1] the letter he received in 1771 from his great-aunt, Lady Leicester of Holkham Hall in the county of Norfolk. Lady Leicester knew, though she was reluctant to admit it, that young Tom Coke would inherit Holkham, and she was concerned that he should prove worthy of his inheritance. She had lost her own son, Edward Coke, in consequence of a career of debauchery. Indeed, it was Edward Coke's death at the early age of thirty-four, without leaving an heir to the great house and estates at Holkham, that had thrown the inheritance at the feet of her great-nephew, young Thomas Coke of Longford. She was resolved that this young man should be saved from a similar fate. The Universities were at a low ebb in both scholarship and morality, and evidently Lady Leicester shared the view of many elders and betters that a course of foreign travel, under suitable guidance, was a desirable substitute. Moreover, her late husband, Lord Leicester, had gone on the Grand Tour to complete his

[1] Thomas William Coke, Earl of Leicester, born in 1754, lived until 1842.

education some sixty years ago, and the whole world knew what had come of that. At the time of her offer of £500 per annum to young Thomas Coke of Longford, providing that he should 'chuse to travel' instead of going to 'one of those Schools of Vice, the Universities', Lady Leicester was still living out her widowhood in that Italianate palace on the edge of the North Sea which her late Lord had built to embody the fine classical taste, and the multitudinous books and manuscripts, pictures and sculpture, acquired during his youthful years of travel. It was surely desirable, on all counts, that the heir to Holkham, the lad from Longford, should follow in the great Lord's footsteps.

Young Tom did not hesitate, more especially as his father offered him an additional £200 per annum if he should decide to accept her ladyship's advice. After a short visit to Holkham, where his great-aunt shook her fist under his nose and assured him that she intended to live as long as possible (actually she died four years later, at the age of seventy-five), he set off for that large and fascinating place known as 'Abroad'. He was only seventeen, but nature and nurture had given him a fine figure and a handsome face. He was to be known, everywhere he went, as 'le bel Anglais'. He was a special favourite with the ladies. Though he was, and for some sixty-six years preferred to remain, simply 'Mr Coke', a commoner, he was nevertheless an aristocrat by birth; though only a country gentleman, albeit one of great expectations, he was also an 'English Milord' with the passport of birth and breeding to the best society of Europe. No doubt there were still elderly persons living beneath the Italian sun who remembered his great-uncle, 'Il Cavaliere Coke', who had passed that way nearly sixty years before, with his coach and six, his plentiful guineas, his attendant carriages and retinue, his chaplain and his grooms, his steward and his valet-de-chambre. That was in the last years of the War of the Spanish Succession and the first years of the Peace of Utrecht, the sunset of the reign of Le Grand Monarque, the age of Queen Anne and Jonathan Swift and the great Duke of Marlborough. Now it was the age of George III, Lord North and John Wilkes, of Richard Arkwright and John Wesley, of Jean-Jacques Rousseau and the Encyclopedia, of Thomas Jefferson and the Rights of Man.

But still the young English Milord went his splendid way, among the deepening shadows of Europe's *ancien régime*, across the fair land of France and under the unblemished skies of Italy. At Turin, the King of Sardinia commanded the ladies of the Court to teach young Mr Coke the cotillion, which he very soon learnt, and assigned to him the honour of dancing with his daughter, the Princess of Savoy, lately affianced to the Comte d'Artois. Mr Coke gallantly rode in the escort of the Princess as far as Cambrai when she set out for her new home. Likewise he danced in Rome at the wedding festivities of the 'Princess of Wales', Louise of Stolberg, bride of the Young Pretender, Charles Edward. The Princess scarcely troubled to conceal her preference for the handsome young Englishman over the no longer very bonny Prince Charlie. She presented Mr Coke with his portrait, painted in fancy dress by the fashionable Battoni, with a statue of the love-lorn Ariadne, bearing a strong likeness to her Royal Highness, in the background. He was most kindly received by the good old Pope, Clement XIV. On his way home he became intimate with the great Chancellor, Prince Kaunitz, in Vienna, not to mention Maria Theresa and the Emperor, afterwards dropping in at Paris, where he enjoyed the early sunshine and gaiety of the newly-ascended Louis XVI and his young Queen, Marie-Antoinette.

It was all very grand, and very expensive. Young Thomas

Coke had a basic allowance of £700 a year, and he was away for three years. Other travellers on the Grand Tour — his great-uncle, 'Il Cavaliere', for instance — commonly spent five times that amount. £10,000 to £15,000, expended over three, four, or five years, was quite common. The Grand Tour was the pastime of a wealthy aristocracy. It justified what may be called 'significant expenditure' — intended to prove that you could afford it in terms of both time and money. To do it on the cheap would have deprived it of its social prestige-value. The elders and betters who footed the bill obviously thought it well worth while. It was a caste-mark within the aristocracy itself. Of course, for a younger son, especially if he were destined for the Church, a period at Oxford or Cambridge, costing only a fraction of the amount, was considered suitable and adequate. But for the young man who was to inherit great properties, and to play his part in politics, war, and diplomacy, it was generally considered essential that he should learn manners and the arts of living in France, that he should acquire a correct taste in the fine arts in Italy, and that he should rub off any remains of English rusticity and insularity in the cosmopolitan Courts and salons and noble houses of the Continent in general. In France he would learn to speak French (it was hoped) like his mother tongue — French, the language of diplomacy, of 'enlightened' philosophy, of universal 'politeness'. There, too, he would learn fencing and horsemanship; ballroom dancing and deportment: the latest style in sartorial elegance. He would practise the social graces in the masked balls and festivities of Venice. In Italy he would learn to admire the domestic architecture of Palladio, Italian marbles, and the stately style of Roman antiquity, along with the great master-painters of the Renaissance.

It would all be quite easy and perfectly delightful, for the English Milord, with his far-famed liberality, was welcome everywhere. Doors opened to him at something less than a knock. Letters of introduction took him at once into the society of those who ruled the world of politics, diplomacy and fashion. His path was smoothed by pre-arrangement, established routes by land and sea, welcoming hostelries, relays of transport laid on in advance — unless he travelled in his own coach, which he often did. Not for him the uncertainties and discomforts experienced by the mere 'Englishman abroad', stumbling along on hired hacks or in the public stage, from one village inn to another, taking pot-luck among the fleas and the burnt *ragoûts*.[1] The first stage, from Dover to Calais, and the penultimate stage over the Alps from France and Switzerland into Italy, were the worst he would encounter. But, once he was at Calais, there was M. Dessein's famous inn, the greatest establishment of its kind in Europe, with its hundred and thirty beds, and more than sixty indoor servants. M. Dessein catered almost exclusively for English travellers, and he ran an excellent post-chaise hire-service. From thence to Amiens, Chantilly and Paris, the route was well worn. After the quite obligatory visits to Versailles, Marly and the Trianon, one might make for Rheims, Châlons and Dijon, or take the direct route through Burgundy to Lyons, and thence along the Rhône to Provence and the Riviera. Crossing the Alps, if one chose to confront the mountainous route from Geneva, was the penultimate stage of peril and discomfort. It could be quite terrifying, as Horace Walpole and Thomas Gray found when they went that way in 1739 on mule-back or in chairs swung on poles. Many travellers in the eighteenth

---

[1] Arthur Young's *Travels in France* provides a vivid account of what this kind of travel was like.

century avoided it, their taste being for cities (preferably Roman cities) rather than unregulated scenery. There was no question of haste, or of making a bee-line across France to Italy. Many months would be spent in touring the cities of the Loire, or Languedoc. One might even venture from Bordeaux to the Pyrenees and into Spain, but this was not usually a success, for the Iberian Peninsula was a place of dirt and discomfort. There were plenty of guide-books to warn and encourage in all this. Thomas Nugent's *Grand Tour* was already on sale by the middle of the century. By 1770 there was *The Gentleman's Guide in his Tour through France*. There was the semi-official *Livre de Poste*, an annual publication, to serve as a kind of Bradshaw to the post-chaise services. Once arrived in Italy, one could go with Jonathan Richardson's *Account* in hand. This little work, published in 1722, was the Baedeker of the Grand Tour for the art treasures of Italy. It would be an exaggeration to say that the Grand Tour ever became a European in-dustry, like modern tourism. All the same, as time went on, and Milord on his Tour became himself one of the sights of Europe, the thing took on some of the character of a ritual, with its well-worn routes, its familiar inns and stages, its classic hunting-grounds for antiques.

When he left England in the summer of 1771, Thomas Coke was a Derbyshire school-boy of seventeen. When he returned in the summer of 1774 he was a man of polished and forthright manners, experienced in the ways of the great world of Courts and Kings, the equal of any gentle-man in Europe. In due course he was to enter into his inheritance at Holkham where he was to reign as the uncrowned king of Norfolk for nearly seventy years. This was the Thomas Coke whose portrait by Gainsborough still hangs in the great Saloon at Holkham. He stands beneath a tree, his game-dogs at his feet, charging his game-gun with a ramrod. He wears loose country clothes of a nonetheless elegant style: double-breasted waistcoat, frilly lace cravat, white buckskin breeches, top-boots, fobs and all. His handsome face and his tall, well-knit figure are only a slightly older version of the beautiful youth who had captured the heart of the Young Pretender's bride at Rome. There is no rusticity here. The great farmer, who taught not only his countrymen but all the world how to farm, was never less than the English Milord who had made the Grand Tour in his youth. The Grand Tour could produce men of fashion, passionate collectors of *objets d'art*, apes of classical antiquity. But it could also produce men. It had a way of setting men free to be themselves.

It would be ridiculous to suppose that Coke of Norfolk would not have become what he was without his youthful experience of Europe. What a young man got out of the Grand Tour depended on what he brought to that experience. Young Coke brought an honest, forthright, uncomplicated nature, an abundant love of life, freshness, courage, an unaffected acceptance of his fellow mortals as God made them, from prince to peasant. His experiences abroad fortified him in these things. His nature preserved him from the affectations of the dilettante, from the veneer of fashion. He seems to have danced his way through France and Italy, although he did all the right things, such as climbing Vesuvius and visiting the excavations at Herculaneum. Like his great-uncle, 'Il Cavaliere Coke', the builder of Holkham, he brought back a number of spoils of the Renaissance and the classical world in his baggage: a bas-relief by Michelangelo, an antique mosaic, a magnificent antique of Minerva, and two fine mosaic tables from Hadrian's villa at Tivoli. All these were to be added to the wonderful collection with which 'Il Cavaliero' had stuffed his palace at Holkham half a century earlier.

He also made away with the famous red opal ring which was discovered in the tomb of the Senator Nonius, a jewel which is mentioned by Pliny and which is said to have been wanted by Antony as a gift for Cleopatra, and valued at somewhere around £20,000. Thomas Coke happened to be there when the tomb was opened. He got hold of it before anyone else had seen it, and he always declined to say what he had paid for it. Thus young Thomas collared his share of classical swag. He could hardly have been said to have made the Grand Tour otherwise. But it was infinitesimal when compared with the amount acquired by 'Il Cavaliere'.

It is difficult to resist the impression that Italy must have been running out of genuine antiques by the seventeen-seventies. For several generations English gentlemen on the Grand Tour had been carrying off marbles, mosaics, pictures and manuscripts. Never had there been such a locust-swarm of art-hungry visitors since the classical mania of the Renaissance. Of course, the middle-men employed by the English buyers coped with the situation with suitable ingenuity, and many a clever fake went back in Milord's luggage to adorn some Palladian mansion set down in England's green and pleasant land. The English art dealer, stationed in Italy, was an expert at 'restoration'. Joseph Nollekens, the great sculptor, made a good thing out of it during his residence in Rome in the seventeen-sixties. 'The patrons of Nollekens,' writes his biographer, 'being characters professing taste and possessing wealth, employed him as a very shrewd collector of antique fragments; some of which he bought on his own account; and, after he had dexterously restored them with heads and limbs, he stained them with tobacco-water, and sold them, sometimes by way of favour, for enormous sums.' On one occasion he bought a head of Minerva from a fellow-dealer, and, having acquired a trunk of Minerva for fifty pounds, invested some twenty pounds in stone and labour in order to produce a complete Minerva, which he sold for a thousand guineas. His repute as a sculptor in his own right served him well in transactions of this kind. He also made quite a profitable side-line out of smuggling Italian silk stockings, lace ruffles and gloves inside the hollow busts which he sent back to England, sealing up their backs with a coating of plaster. 'There,' he once said to Lord Mansfield, pointing to the cast of his celebrated bust of Laurence Sterne, the novelist; 'there, do you know, that busto, my Lord, held my lace ruffles that I went to Court in when I came from Rome.'

Whether the English gentleman on the Grand Tour, or doing business with agents in Italy after his return, got genuine value for his money, or was fobbed off with a fake, largely depended upon the extent of his own knowledge and cultivation. 'Professing taste and possessing wealth' implies a nice distinction, and undoubtedly there were many who possessed more money than sense. But, after all, the Grand Tour was, at its best, an educational enterprise. It quite often served as an alternative to a university education, and it might include within its itinerary a period of residence at a foreign seat of learning. Thus, Thomas Coke, Earl of Leicester, 'Il Cavaliere', was sent abroad to complete his education at the University of Turin, and the Grand Tour was intended to be an enlargement of this primary academic experience. This young man supplies us, indeed, with the example *par excellence* of that combination of wealth and taste and scholarly interests which alone could make the Grand Tour a thoroughly profitable aristocratic enterprise. Although he was little more than fifteen when he set out, he took with him not only a train of carriages and a retinue of servants,

but a keen intelligence and a passionate devotion to literature. He was no mere collector of classical loot, a snob-
victim of sharks and swindlers, but a scholar. He read his
classical authors methodically as he travelled. He specialized in the works of, and anything connected with, the
great Roman historian, Livy. He collected the works of
most of the great Italian painters of the Renaissance, from
Michelangelo to Titian. His knowledge and perspicacity,
not to mention his great wealth, enabled him to purchase
genuine, and genuinely beautiful, examples of classical
sculpture. True, he had the great good fortune to travel in
Italy with the supreme arbiter of classical taste and wisdom, Lord Burlington; and for a time, at least, he travelled
in the company of William Kent, the most celebrated
architect in the Palladian style. For many years after his
return to England he was engaged in the planning, building and adornment of the great house on the coast of Norfolk which still remains, somewhat incongruously perhaps,
the finest monument to the art of Palladio among the
country-houses of England. Holkham Hall might equally
well be described as England's memorial of the Grand
Tour, or of the education of English aristocratic taste.

Why this cult of the ancient civilizations of Greece[1] and
Rome? In the great days of the Grand Tour — the first
half of the eighteenth century — educated Englishmen
believed themselves to be living in a second Augustan age.
The wars of religion were over. Civil strife in its bloodier
forms was coming to an end. England was believed to have
arrived at a satisfactory and stable compromise in civil
government and religious toleration by the Glorious
Revolution of 1688–9. The great figures were no longer

[1] Very few travellers penetrated into Greece, which was under Turkish
rule and infested by brigands as well as fleas. The best of Greek culture was
thought to be accessible in Italy.

Cromwell and Milton, but Walpole and Pope. It was possible to believe that civility and politeness were fast reaching the point where they might be seen to link hands with the last great ages of moderation, equability and peace — the ages of the Emperor Augustus and of the Antonines — after so many centuries of 'Gothic barbarism', unrelieved save for the brief glory of the Italian Renaissance. Moreover, the Augustan age believed in 'Europe', and in a single 'European civilization' historically bounded by the frontiers of the Roman Empire. Edmund Burke was to express this belief in the basic unity of 'Europe' when he wrote in 1796, in his *Letters on a Regicide Peace*, of 'the similitude throughout Europe of religion, laws and manners'. Europe, he declared, was something more than a mere aggregate of nations. It was a single commonwealth, 'virtually one great state having the same basis of general law, with some diversity of provincial customs and local establishments'. No citizen of Europe could be altogether an exile in any part of it. 'When a man travelled or resided abroad for health, pleasure, business or necessity from his own country, he never felt himself quite abroad.' No doubt there is some exaggeration in this, as there is in most of Burke's nostalgic statements. But there is some truth in it, especially at the higher social levels. There certainly was something that might be called an Aristocratic International in the eighteenth century, however little of it there was among peoples in general. 'Fraternity', one of the watchwords of the French Revolution, was far less in evidence among democrats than among aristocrats, as any study of the *émigré* movement clearly reveals. To put it at the lowest — the level of mere self-preservation — all aristocracies, in all ages, are primarily concerned to keep the world safe for aristocracy. The qualities they will cherish are necessarily the qualities of stability, moderation, restraint: the qualities we sum up in the vague term 'classical'. Roman antiquity embodied them all.

Thus the cult of classical antiquity was as natural to the aristocracy of the eighteenth century as the cult of the Middle Ages was to become in the century that followed. It was as natural for the aristocrat on the Grand Tour to visit Herculaneum and to bring home marbles and mosaics from the disinterred temples and palaces of classical antiquity as it was for the nineteenth-century tourist to go and view fair Melrose aright by visiting it by pale moonlight, or for the tourist of the twentieth century to bring home a camera full of snaps of romantic scenery. These last are representative of the cult of the romantic view of life, natural to middle-class or working-class democracy. The aristocrat on the Grand Tour disliked the wild and unregulated features of 'romantic' scenery, or nature untamed by the hand of man. It is said that Lord Chesterfield used to draw down the blinds of his carriage when he came in sight of the Alps. The poet, Thomas Gray, as early as 1739, could record on his journey among the mountains to the Grande Chartreuse: 'not a precipice, not a torrent, not a cliff, but is pregnant with religion and poetry.' Gray heralded the romantic response. Wordsworth, writing in *The Prelude* of his youthful tramp to Italy as an undergraduate in 1790, was to celebrate his first view of Mont Blanc and the majesty of the mountains as affording man sublime insight into the heart of truth. Chesterfield was an aristocrat, Gray was the son of a scrivener, Wordsworth liked to think of himself as the adopted son of Cumberland peasants. With these three we can see tourism transformed from a stately progress in search of classical antiquity to a hike in search of the beauties of nature.

The Grand Tour had always its critics. Criticism

generally turned upon its utility as an educational device
for the youth of an essentially commercial nation like the
English. Was it proper that young men should spend their
formative years frivolling at the courts of Europe, staring
at Palladian façades, or chasing after antiques? Certainly
not, Adam Smith declared unequivocally in *The Wealth of
Nations* (1776). The popularity of the Grand Tour as an
alternative to a University education simply indicated
how low the Universities had fallen. 'Nothing but the
discredit into which the Universities are allowing themselves to fall, could ever have brought into repute so very
absurd a practice. . . .' A young man who went abroad at
seventeen or eighteen simply returned home, at one-and-
twenty, some three or four years older. Foreign languages?
He might have picked up a smattering, 'seldom sufficient
to enable him either to speak or write them with propriety'.
Manners? 'He commonly returns home more conceited,
more unprincipled, more dissipated, and more incapable
of any serious application, either to study or to business,
than he could well have become in so short a time had he
lived at home.' Beyond sight of his parents, 'spending in
the most frivolous dissipation the most precious years of
his life', every useful habit formed in his earliest years
becomes weakened or effaced. As one might expect, the
keynote of Adam Smith's comments is the test of utility —
utility defined according to the standards of a man of
business in the dawn of the Industrial Revolution.

Not that the application of such standards had to wait
upon the increasing speed of industrial and commercial
change in eighteenth-century England. John Locke was
credited with holding similar views nearly a hundred years
before Adam Smith published his famous book. In 1764
Richard Hurd, Bishop of Worcester, published his *Dialogues on the Uses of Foreign Travel*, considered as a Part of

an English Gentleman's Education. Hurd put the argument into the mouths of Lord Shaftesbury and Mr Locke in a debate supposed to have taken place in 1700. While Shaftesbury, the dilettante philosopher and aesthete, champions foreign travel with all the customary arguments for the Grand Tour as a mode of higher education, Locke enters his caveats very much in the style of Adam Smith. He deplores the waste of time, the superficiality of the accomplishments attained, the lack of homely solidity and moral strength, the smattering and the premature sophistication. In the Courts of Europe a young man learns servility rather than liberty, manners (of a kind) instead of sound morals, the civilization of gentlemen rather than the culture of men. Better a modest home-bred youth than a travelled and over-confident booby. And if knowledge of the world is in question, how much of the world is constituted by 'Europe'? Locke would retort upon those who advocated the Grand Tour as a means to know human nature: 'That, to study Human Nature to purpose, a Traveller must enlarge his circuit beyond the bounds of Europe. He must go and catch Her undressed, nay quite naked in North America and at the Cape of Good Hope', not to mention China and Japan. 'These, my Lord, are the proper scenes for the Philosopher, for the citizen of the world, to expatiate in. The tour of Europe is a paltry thing; a tame, uniform, unvaried prospect; which affords nothing but the same polished manners and artificial politeness, scarcely diversified enough to take, or merit our attention.' And if it is objected that these wider scenes 'impose too great a task on our inquisitive Traveller, my next advice is, That he stay at home; read Europe in the mirror of his own country. . . .' Anyway, what are books of travel for?

Needless to say, there was never the slightest likelihood

of this sober, not to say sombre, advice being taken. 'The English look on their isle as a prison,' wrote the Abbé Le Blanc in 1745, 'and the first use they make of their love of liberty is to get out of it.' Indeed, their inveterate habit of flitting around Europe had been a favourite subject for satire ever since the sixteenth century, when the 'Italianate Englishman', with his affected manners, speech and dress came uproariously upon the stage in the plays of Shakespeare, Ben Jonson, and many more. By the eighteenth century, when the habit had become institutionalized by a wealthy aristocracy, mere mockery was not enough, in fact it was out of place. A more constructive style of criticism was needed, something more positive than the rather cross-patch animadversions that such utilitarian critics as Locke and Richard Hurd and Adam Smith could supply. If the practice could not be checked by mockery or outright condemnation, it might be possible to transform it by instruction, to turn it to socially useful purposes. This was attempted as early as 1758 by Dean Tucker in his *Instructions for Travellers*, with its sub-title: A Plan for improving the Moral and Political Theory of Trade and Taxes by means of Travelling. The Dean began by enumerating the motives for travel as they were usually stated by the advocates of the Grand Tour: the desire to improve one's taste for the fine arts, to obtain a reputation as a man of 'virtu and elegant taste', and to rub off local prejudices and acquire an enlarged and impartial view of men and things. He then proceeds to enumerate the more foolish motives favoured by the critics: the desire to acquire foreign airs, and to adorn one's 'dear person' with fine clothes and the newest fashions; to visit Italy and Greece[1] 'out of a kind of enthousiastic reverence for Classic Ground' to pay literary adoration to 'the very Rubbish of an

[1] See footnote to p. 131.

Ancient City'; and to dispel the boredom of 'those who are tired of living at home and can afford to make themselves as ridiculous everywhere as they please.' Tucker recommends a preliminary tour of one's own country, and then a course of solid reading in theology (in order to guard against the infection of popery), political philosophy, and political economy. 'The ignorant traveller is of all Beings the most contemptible.' Lacking a sound instruction, he will not know what to look out for. The Dean supplies a long list of questions to which the instructed traveller should try to find answers. They include everything from comparative manuring of different soils, the progress of invention, and the securities afforded for safeguarding civil and political rights and religious toleration, down to the number of loaded waggons that pass along the roads and the system of taxation.

Evidently, the beau-idéal of Dean Tucker would have been a political economist, a utilitarian, and something of a bore. Arthur Young, while he was never a bore, was to fulfil most of his demands. Young's *Travels in France*, on the eve of the Revolution, answers most of the questions outlined by the Dean. The Suffolk farmer was the very type of 'the man with a notebook', and he is only the greatest of a multitude who travelled for information about existing conditions. But Arthur Young's travels were not the Grand Tour. Indeed, Dean Tucker's adjurations, if acted upon, would have turned the Grand Tour into something quite different. In fact, it never did turn into anything different. For long enough yet, the aristocracy, great and small, was to go its more or less splendid and carefree way. Well into the seventeen-sixties the little Scots laird, James Boswell (or 'Baron Boswell', as he chose to be known while travelling in Germany), was jaunting his way to immortality without a thought for political economy, or indeed any other kind of economy, while the old laird of Auchinleck, back home in Scotland, groaned under the financial burden and commanded him to return:

> This much I can say, that you have spent a vast deal of money . . . much beyond what the sons of gentlemen near double my estate have spent on such a tour. . . . You have had full opportunity to be satisfied that pageantry, civil and ecclesiastic, gives no entertainment to thinking men, and that there is no end nor use of strolling through the world to see sights before unseen, whether of man, beasts, birds, or things, and I hope will return with a proper taste and relish for your own country. . . .

The most that Lord Auchinleck could hope for, he said, was that young James would return 'a man of knowledge, of gravity and modesty, intent upon being useful in life. If this be so,' he added, much after the style of John Locke or Adam Smith, 'your travelling will be a little embellishment to the more essential talents. . . .' On no account should James linger in Paris on his way home. 'There is nothing to be learned by travelling in France.' Three or four days in Paris would be ample. Lord Auchinleck was writing in August, 1765. James Boswell arrived at Dover in the following February, having seduced Rousseau's mistress *en route*. Grand Tour or no Grand Tour, Boswell would always have been Boswell.

It was not until many years after James Boswell was back in Scotland that Frederick Hervey, fourth Earl of Bristol and Lord Bishop of Derry, drew to the close of a Grand Tour that had lasted half a life-time. Bowling along the roads of France and Italy, leaving a trail of Hotels Bristol in his wake, he was for many years the best-known traveller and collector in Europe. In 1792 he began to build a splendid repository for his treasures at Ickworth, the old home of the Herveys, in Suffolk. With its pillared portico, its vast rotunda, its curving corridor-rooms flanking the central dome and running out to east and west wings on either side, it was to have been a house to rival Holkham itself. Unfortunately, the French Revolution broke out in 1789, and in 1798 the armies of the Revolution entered Rome. History, as Edward Gibbon discovered when he fled from Lausanne before the self-same intrusion in 1793, was still going on. The French confiscated the Lord Bishop's treasures, and the Lord Bishop himself spent nine months in prison in Milan. He died in Rome in 1803, and Ickworth House, minus his treasures, was to remain a gorgeous and unfinished monument to the Grand Tour *manqué*. Something new had come into the world, as Goethe observed of the battle of Valmy: the first of the 'wars of the people'. The little wars of the eighteenth century, those 'temperate and indecisive contests' of the kings, had scarcely affected the Grand Tour. 'Il Cavaliere Coke' had set out while the War of the Spanish Succession was still unconcluded. Horace Walpole came home from his travels nearly two years after his country had gone to war with Spain, nine months after Frederick the Great invaded Silesia, and all that appears to have worried him was the possibility of his being captured by Catalan pirates on his journey in a felucca from Genoa to Antibes. Laurence Sterne, ordered south for his health in the winter of 1762, was able quite easily to travel through the dominions of the King of France, with whom his Britannic Majesty was still at war. As late as 1790 young Wordsworth and his friend Jones, returning from their tramp to Italy,

> . . . cross'd the Brabant armies on the fret
> For battle in the cause of Liberty.

This happy state of things, when wars were still kingly contests and not yet ideological fights to the death, was fast coming to an end. From 1793 to 1815, with only a brief period of intermission after the Peace of Amiens, the errant English were to be shut up in their island. Grand Tours were confined to soldiers and sailors, travelling under conditions of some squalor and considerable danger.

All the same, it would be misleading to describe the Grand Tour as a victim of the French Revolution. For some time past, travel had been undergoing social change. More and more people of middle-class origin had been making some show of 'tourism'. The very word suggests rather an alternative than a transformation. These people certainly went on tour, but they did it on the cheap, and quite without grandeur. Thomas Patch, a Londoner of obscure parentage who was to become a well-known etcher and engraver at Florence, is said to have hitch-hiked his way to Rome some time before 1750. 'Dr Viper', or the quarrelsome Philip Thicknesse, turned continental travel into a family picnic. True, his travels were confined to France, but he certainly showed what could be done to adapt tourism to the income of a family man of limited means. Disappointed of a legacy for which he had waited hopefully for some years, he decided that he could live and educate his children more cheaply in France. On his second journey, in 1776, he packed his family into a heavy French cabriolet at Dessein's hotel at Calais, along with pots and pans and musical instruments, his wife's parakeet and his own pet monkey, and set out for Rheims, Dijon, Lyons and Nîmes, and the Mediterranean shore. They took their meals by the roadside, picnicking on one occasion under the arches of the Pont du Gard. While the kettle boiled for tea, father would play tunes on his guitar, much to the delight of the peasants, who 'danced in a manner not to be seen in England'. Jocko, the monkey, dressed in French jackboots, and with his hair *en queue*, rode much of the way postilion on the carriage-horse, a sight which put 'whole towns in motion . . .' This was certainly not the classical Grand Tour. It was tourism *à la* Swiss Family Robinson, the descent from the sublime to the ridiculous. With Wordsworth and Jones tramping from Calais to Lake Maggiore in the summer vacation of 1790, the age of the hiker was well within sight. All that was needed, now, was the steamship, the railway, and the family car. The Grand Tour could scarcely adapt itself to the Age of the Common Man. The story that began with Thomas Coke ends with Thomas Cook.

SUGGESTIONS FOR FURTHER READING

Stirling, A. M. M., *Coke of Norfolk and his Friends*, Lane, 1908. (Chapters 2, 5 & 6).

Maxwell, C., *The English Traveller in France, 1698–1815*, Routledge, 1932.

Ketton-Cremer, R. W., *Horace Walpole*, Duckworth, 1940.

Boswell on the Grand Tour, edited by F. A. Pottle, 2 vols., Heinemann, 1955.

Nugent, T., *The Grand Tour*, 4 vols., London, 1749.

Tucker, J., *Instructions for Travellers*, London, 1757.

Dialogues on the uses of foreign travel, etc., edited by R. Hurd, London, 1764.

The Listener, Dec. 31, 1959, Jan. 7 and 14, 1960. (Reprint of four talks under the heading 'The Grand Tour', by J. H. Plumb and N. McKendrick.)

VIII

The Growth of Literary Taste in the Eighteenth Century

by RACHEL TRICKETT

THE changes that came over English literature in the eighteenth century were to some extent the result of a complex mingling of political, social, and philosophical causes. But none of these causes, singly or united, can completely account for the shifts of sensibility, the variations of taste, and the developments of mood, which make up the prevailing temper of the period. Literature is far too subtle and intricate a mode of interpreting reality to be readily explicable in these terms. It has its own private life as well as its relation to the public experience of the age, and a study of the literature of any period must take into account both these elements. Yet it is true that in no other previous age had literature been so closely bound up with public life as it was from 1660 onwards. The great change in tone and spirit came with the Restoration; after 1688 such alterations as took place were in the nature of slow and gradual modifications of the new mood which first became apparent with the return of Charles II.

Dryden, who saw himself as 'betwixt two ages cast, The first of this and hindmost of the last', was yet proudly conscious of his role as the leader of a new movement which was refining and civilizing the rough extravagances of taste and conduct of an earlier age. In his complimentary epistle To My Dear Friend, Mr. Congreve, he described the influence of the Restoration on the manners of society and the style of the new comic drama it patronized:

> And thus, when Charles return'd, our Empire stood,
> Like Janus, he the stubborn Soil manur'd,
> With Rules of Husbandry the Rankness cur'd:
> Tam'd us to Manners, when the Stage was rude,
> And boistrous English wit with Art indu'd.

A few lines later he admitted, however, that though much had been gained, something had been lost:

> Our Age was cultivated thus at length,
> But what we gain'd in Skill we lost in Strength.

This was evidently true of the comedy of the period, which reflected the manners of a very narrow circle of Court wits and their town imitators. It was true, again, of the pallid imitations of classical literature, where only too often strength was polished into weakness. But there was one kind of writing of which it was conspicuously untrue. In satire 'boistrous English wit' was far from dead, and satire was the most vital and popular poetic form of the period. Traditionally satire had always been familiar, rough and vigorous: polish was not its aim; realism and honesty were. The satirist, alert to the temper of his time, observed keenly and commented with passion. He seldom pretended to detachment; sometimes he might even deny the need for skill or technique, claiming that the force of his anger carried him along:

> Nor needs there Art, or Genius here to use,
> Where Indignation can create a Muse.[1]

These lines echo the spirit of Juvenal which had always been more congenial to English poets than that of the milder Horace, and Restoration satirists, for all their

[1] Oldham; Prologue to the *Satyrs Against the Jesuits*.

admiration of Horace, wrote more often with the savage indignation and the 'surly virtue' of his successor. In Dryden's case this was due to a purely personal preference for Juvenal's more energetic style:

> Juvenal is of a more vigorous and masculine wit. . . . I have the pleasure of concernment in all he says. He drives his reader along with him.[1]

But other satirists, whatever their considered judgments on style, felt the need to write as if they and their readers were deeply involved in the subject of the poem. Though Horace was complimented and recommended for an easy style that 'healed with morals what it hurt with wit', his manner was scarcely suitable for the rough and tumble of political controversy with which Restoration satire was so intimately concerned. Butler's *Hudibras*, Dryden's *Absalom and Achitophel* and *The Medal*, Marvell's *Last Instructions to A Painter* and Oldham's *Satyrs Against the Jesuits* are all vehemently topical, while the collection of *Poems On Affairs of State* (1697), an anthology of works 'from the Time of Oliver Cromwell to the Abdication of King James II', is crowded with political lampoons, heavy argumentative satires, libellous squibs and broadsides, and serious attempts to serve the cause of one party or another in verse. Poets, infected by the disputatious mood of the time, and for the purely practical purposes of earning a living, felt it necessary to show where their allegiance lay. It had become clear during the Civil War that topical pamphlets could be a powerful influence on public opinion, and Restoration poets were not slow to seize the chance of profiting by this lesson. Though the most obvious course a poet could take to make money was writing for the stage, he might usefully

---

[1] Dryden; *Essay on Satire*, prefaced to the translations of Juvenal and Persius.

make himself known and keep himself busy by engaging in the political struggles of the day and hiring out his talents. When the Whig Parliament of 1679 refused to renew the Press Act the result was a war of pamphlets which became a war of poems, too. The satires produced at the height of the Exclusion-Bill agitation were written in haste in the heat of the moment, and few of them achieved anything near the gravity and decorum of Dryden's *Absalom and Achitophel*; they were closer in tone to the angry invective of *The Medal*. Yet even these display something of the force, the well-observed detail of contemporary events and characters, which belong to topical satire. Popular and ephemeral though they were, poems of this kind helped to bring a new and authentic note of realism into English verse.

It is a curious fact that the correct and stylized manner of non-satiric Augustan poetry was gradually being established in this turbulent period. More serious or more leisured poets were anxious to insist on literary tradition and continuity in a time of such violent change and transition. They began to examine their technique in the light of critical precepts and of the practice of the admired ancients whose works had survived as models of wit, intelligibility and nature. Alongside this conservative impulse existed a more immediate desire to purify the language and make it more sociable and communicative — a language which was recognizable as the speech of a man talking to men in the commonest and yet the most civilized sense. The satirist inevitably adopted a tone of good fellowship and honest forthrightness; it was one of his most successful techniques of persuasion. But the courtier or the town wit, for a more exclusive reason — to advertise his membership of a polite and fashionable circle — tried to reproduce in his poems the accents of the man of the world. For him the Horatian style was the ideal medium.

The relaxed and easy manner of the verse epistle, the 'slip-shod muse', suggested confidence, good-breeding and intimacy. The same informal elegance characterizes the best lyrics of the period, where ingenious metaphysical conceits or ornate Renaissance images are exchanged for a new ideal of what is natural and polite. 'Nature's chief masterpiece is writing well', the Earl of Mulgrave observed in his *Essay Upon Poetry* (1682), and writing well meant paying your reader the compliment of addressing him intelligibly and assuming that you shared the same tastes and inhabited the same small world.

Such was the literary situation towards the end of the seventeenth century — on the one hand a vigorous popular tradition of satire and argumentative poetry on topical matter; on the other the self-consciously cultivated style which reflected the tastes and manners of a limited fashionable coterie. By 1690 most young men coming down from the University with the intention of setting up for a poet were more attracted by the latter. Like Prior, they may have begun by practising their wit in satire against other writers of the time, but they were quick to perceive the dangers of entering the field of political journalism. Even when the Press Act was finally repealed in 1695 there was no great outpouring of party verse. A change in taste had gradually taken place. These new writers were keenly aware of how precarious the life of the professional poet had been in the Restoration. Cowley, used to the gentler literary climate of an earlier age, had hardly survived his disappointment after the return of Charles II, and had died in melancholy and embittered poverty. Ambition must be made of sterner stuff, but even a poet with Dryden's skill in steering his career through the quicksands of change might find himself, as Dryden did, deprived of fortune and place when one government gave way to another. A writer who depended on public favour could not even be sure of success if he adopted the attitude of Elkanah Settle, the perfect Vicar of Bray of the literary world, who turned his coat with every shift of power to secure his meagre post of City Poet. Johnson, in his *Life of Pope*, tells how Settle perfected the art of literary salesmanship, having always to hand an elegy or epithalamium with blanks to be filled in by the names of the highest bidders. Settle's history was a moral lesson to the young poets of the age. Dryden's Doeg, he began as a popular dramatist and well-known public songster, and ended up not only as the victim of another great satirist, Pope, but miserably reduced to playing the part of the dragon in a Smithfield spectacle he had organized. Prior in his *Satyr Upon the Poets* singles him out as a warning:

> Recanting Settle brings the tuneful Ware
> Which wiser Smithfield damn'd to Sturbridge Fair;
> Protests his Tragedies and Libels fail
> To yield him Paper, Penny-loaves and Ale,
> And bids our Youth, by his Example fly
> The love of Politicks and Poetry.[1]

Prior himself carefully avoided this predicament. In his *Essay on Learning* he remarks that anyone who hopes to achieve security and make his way in the world had better steer clear of satire:

> I did not launch out much into Satyr; which, however agreable for the present to Writers or Incouragers of it does in time do neither of them good, considering the Uncertainty of Fortune, and the various change of Ministry, where every Man as he resents may Punish in his turn of greatness.[2]

Instead of satire, imitations of the ancients, translations,

[1] Matthew Prior; *Literary Works*, ed. Wright and Spears, Oxford, 1959, Vol. I, p. 28.
[2] *Ibid.*, Vol. I, p. 583.

pastoral lyrics of frigid artificiality and rhetorical odes were now the exercises to which the aspiring poet turned. He could be better paid for a panegyric than for a lampoon, and a translation might bring him to the notice of some politician who needed an educated man to fill a minor post in the government. Prior was made an ambassador; Walsh, Pope's early friend and adviser, was a Whig member of parliament, while Addison reached the heights of a Secretary of State. A new age had clearly set in for the professional author. Nor were these new poets members of the brilliant circle of Court wits. They were willing to accept the patronage of the nobility — and most of the Restoration wits who survived, like Dorset, Halifax and Mulgrave, became the literary patrons of the eighteenth century — but they themselves were typical of a different section of society. From various backgrounds, they were mostly educated men, but like Congreve they preferred to be considered as gentlemen rather than as authors, and they were very much aware of their position and their opportunities in a more secure and orderly world. The Revolution of 1688 had brought about the prospect of a literary settlement as well as a political one. An anonymous satirist, in a poem *The Country Parson's Advice to those little Scribblers, who pretend to write better sense than Great Secretaries* (1706),[1] reflects the scorn of the new society for the Grub Street hacks and even those journalists who pandered to the new and quieter taste for translation:

> Libels that raise the trembling Poet's fears
> And set Mankind together by the Ears,
> These to avoid, in dull Translations Trade,
> *Bowyer* and *Savage* and *Oldmixon* read;
> Or deal in News, and write whate'er you will,
> But see you Scribble on the right Side still.

[1] *Poems On Affairs of State*, Vol. 4, p. 63.

The truth was that country parsons, country squires, men about town and city merchants had lost their taste for dispute and for setting mankind by the ears. Temporarily they had settled their differences and were anxious to relish the new sense of peace and order. They disliked the disputatious poetry of the Restoration, but most of them felt only a tepid interest in the translations, verse treatises and uninspired lyrics that were being turned out in the meantime. The old satire had been scandalous but entertaining; the new reputable verse was frankly dull. They felt the need for something that came home more genuinely to the business and bosom of every man: a kind of literature which would be lively and topical but respectable and exemplary at the same time. It was this need which Addison, with his extraordinary genius for tact, taste and ingenuity, came forward to fill.

The Tatler and *The Spectator* seemed to Dr Johnson to have filled the same function as the courtesy books of the Italian Renaissance. Up to this time in England he says 'no writers had yet undertaken to reform either the savageness of neglect or the impertinency of civility'.[1] Dryden, we have seen, claimed that the comic dramatists had achieved the first, but in doing so they had certainly fallen into the 'impertinence of civility'. Though treatises and satires had guided men's opinions, there had been no *arbiter elegantiarum* until Addison, largely, perhaps, because society had not felt that it wanted one. But Addison's aim of bringing philosophy down from the schools to the coffee-houses was entirely in tune with the needs of his age. He reproduced in prose the elegant accents of the Horatian poet; he turned his attention to everyday affairs as seriously as before him authors had considered men's moral, religious and political duties. As seriously, but more

[1] Johnson, *Lives of the Poets*, World's Classics, Vol. I, p. 423.

engagingly, more intimately, and with his eye on a wider public. Instead of violently satirizing women's fashions in dress and décor, for instance, he persuasively rallied them and tried to enlarge their tastes and interests. He showed women, and men too, what to look for in Milton's poems; how to enjoy the pleasures of the country or the rational delights of social intercourse; he told them how they should talk and what they could talk about. In familiar epistles and imaginary episodes he presented the embarrassments, the difficulties and dilemmas of everyday life, and delighted a public which responded at once to the novel pleasure of seeing their own environment, their own problems and ways of life, so authentically yet so elegantly reflected in literature. With the help of Steele, the gentle, humorous and sympathetic observer of common life, Addison found a new way of interpreting the old aim of literature — to instruct and please at the same time.

The popularity of these moral essays was enormous. Readers could not have enough of the tactful flattery of essays which were directly addressed to them for their amusement and for their profit. They began to feel that it was both fashionable and worth while to be civil, cultivated and lightly learned. When Johnson looked back over the changes in the tone of society during the eighteenth century, he considered that many of the most important of them were due to Addison's influence:

That general knowledge which now circulates in common talk, was in his time, rarely to be found. Men not professing learning were not ashamed of ignorance; and in the female world any acquaintance with books was distinguished only to be censured. His purpose was to infuse literary curiosity, by gentle and unsuspected conveyance, into the gay, the idle and the wealthy; he therefore presented knowledge in the most alluring form, not lofty and austere, but accessible and familiar. When he shewed them their defects, he shewed them likewise that they might be supplied. His attempt succeeded; enquiry was awakened, and comprehension expanded. An emulation of intellectual elegance was excited, and from his time to our own, life has been gradually exalted and conversation purified and enlarged.[1]

But though the readers and writers of the eighteenth century were keenly aware of how much they had improved on their inheritance, they were still the direct descendants of the Restoration. That very spirit which demanded a literature dealing with life and common experience had grown up in the more unruly period, when men were first beginning to look for a plain style and rational, realistic subject matter.

It is a commonplace of literary criticism that the use of literature as propaganda, the development of the Royal Society with its need for a style that was clear and analytical, and the increasing public for poetry and prose, led to a shift from figurative to plain perspicuous language in the late seventeenth century. Sprat, Bishop of Rochester and the historian of the Royal Society, inveighed against the dangers of metaphor which concealed simple truth. In execrable pindarics, he praised Cowley for having rejected fabulous frivolities and brought a new seriousness into verse:

> Poets till now deserv'd Excuse not Praise,
> Till now the Muses liv'd in Taverns and the Bays
> That they were truly Trees did shew
> Because by sucking Liquor they did only grow.
> Verses were counted Fiction, and a Lye
> The very Nature of Good Poetry.
> He was a Poet that cou'd speak least Truth:
> Sober and grave men scorn'd the Name
> Which once was thought the greatest Fame.[2]

[1] Johnson, *op. cit.*, p. 463.
[2] *The Minor Poets or the Works of the most Celebrated Authors*, 1751, Vol. 2, p. 356.

When sober and grave men began to doubt the validity of the idea of truth on which the poetry of the past had been raised, the time had certainly come for a change in style and subject matter. The old way of looking at truth as if it were inseparable from the images, the great formal conventions, and the myths in which it could be expressed, was dying gradually throughout the seventeenth century. That integrated picture of reality which had grown up from a union of medieval Aristotelianism and Renaissance neo-Platonism fell a victim to the restlessness of the age, the urgency of political and religious disputes, and the experience of civil war. At the Restoration men were examining the premisses of their thought and behaviour more critically and experimentally. The poetry and the prose of the period turned its back on what was now condemned as 'false fabling'. Figurative language was reserved for the high style of panegyric, and as that form became more and more debased the style too was discredited. By the eighteenth century it was a mark of insincerity and indifference to truth. Thomas Tickell, Addison's protégé and Pope's rival as a translator of Homer, hailed the accession of George I in these significant terms:

> When Brunswick first appear'd each honest Heart
> Intent on verse, disdain'd the rules of Art,
> For him the Songsters, in unmeasur'd Odes
> Debas'd Alcides and dethron'd the Gods. . . .
> Exploded fancies! which in vain deceive
> While the mind nauseates what she can't believe.[1]

It was a point of poetic faith for Pope's contemporaries to hold that 'honest hearts' as opposed to mere songsters were bound by a strict and literal interpretation of the truth, since 'the mind nauseates what she can't believe'.

[1] *Minor Poets*, Vol. 2, p. 208: 'The Royal Progress'.

Johnson's notorious attacks on the pastoral convention and the use of mythology in verse were wholly in keeping with the better literary judgment of his time. Truthfulness of material was the sole guarantee of sincerity, and sincerity distinguished the dedicated poet from the hired hack, especially sincerity in praise. Pope himself epitomizes this view in his life and his work. 'Unplac'd, unpension'd, no man's heir or slave', he stands out from the Grub Street race he so bitterly attacked in *The Dunciad* by his independence and his refusal to compromise with the strict demands of honesty. His muse searches out the real virtues of a Man of Ross, or celebrates the nobility of a statesman out of place, like Harley after his downfall.

The taste for accuracy and truth as a badge of integrity was shared by poets and their readers in the eighteenth century. It was connected, too, with their passion for history, for recorded facts which would present the truth about the past. History in the Renaissance period had been looked upon as an exemplary discipline in which legendary characters and events might be of greater value than actual ones, since they could more perfectly illustrate ideal truth. The Augustans believed that history was only exemplary because it dealt with actual and verifiable facts from which the truth could be learned. Statesmen were beginning to look back for historical precedent and justification for their policies, and men were developing the taste for tracing the causes and effects of action in real past examples, and for looking to history as a record of human experience and a guide to human conduct. Historical surveys in verse of the growth of an art, like Dryden's *Epistles* to Congreve and Kneller, were admired as gratifying accounts of the progress of civilization. Satirists and didactic poets were to be found using historical analogies to support their case. History itself was becoming

F

a popular literary form. The memoirs of public figures like Temple, or longer studies like Clarendon's *History of the Great Rebellion* or Burnet's *History of his own Time*, were read eagerly by men anxious to decide for themselves the truth about the confused political circumstances through which they and their fathers had passed. Such was the popularity of the form that hack journalists like Oldmixon (one of Pope's victims in *The Dunciad*) turned their hand to it. Oldmixon's *History of England*, with its violently Whiggish interpretation of the events leading up to and following the Revolution, was widely read throughout the eighteenth century, even when the taste for disinterested and more philosophical histories had brought into prominence the work of men like Hume and Robertson. In his criticism, Oldmixon lays down rules for the writing of history,[1] that he had taken from Rapin who, having come to England with William III, set out to use the existing documents which were officially under the control of the Historiographer Royal (in this case the notorious Rymer) and himself produced a History of England. 'Disons la vérité sans commentaires, si nous avons la force d'esprit pour cela',[2] wrote Rapin of the art of the historian. It was an art which came near to the eighteenth century's view of the moral satirist — the recorder of his age. But the truth told by the satirist was not to be told without commentary.

Pope, of all the Augustans, reflects most subtly this love of truth, of historical fact, and of sincerity. His satire was topical, but, unlike that of Dryden and his contemporaries, it had a moral context which gave it detachment. He sees the follies of his age, the corruption of the administration,

[1] Oldmixon; *Essay on Criticism as it regards Design, Thought, and Expression in Prose and Verse*, 1728.
[2] Rapin; *Les Réflections sur l'Histoire*, XXI.

the debasement of literature, the love of money and of place, against the great perspective of moral truth and the record of the past. Horace provided him with a norm, but the truth about life, and 'the black fear of death which saddens all', was the back-cloth against which he saw the present. To Pope history was of two kinds — the facts of the present, and the record of common experience which had come down from the ancients to the poets of his day. He meant to 'publish the present age', but his task was more complicated than that of earlier satirists, since the present age with its new tastes and ideals demanded more than a party point of view. Pope was, if anything, a Tory when he wrote his *Moral Essays* and his *Imitations of Horace*, but he was eager to show that he was no party satirist. When he attacks the abuses of wealth he is as quick to 'bare the mean heart that lurks beneath a star' as to ridicule the *nouveau riche* Sir Balaam, the city merchant whose Whig forebears had been the butt of Dryden's scorn. Pope may have agreed with Bolingbroke in condemning the Whigs for having created a monied interest to counterbalance the influence of the landed aristocracy,[1] but he maintained the impartiality of the moral poet in his satires. He is not afraid to praise a Lord Mayor, just as in his private life he was not ashamed of his friendship with Hugh and Slingsby Bethel, the descendants of Dryden's Shimei. His attacks were on general corruption, and though Walpole was inevitably his whipping boy in the matter of public bribery, Pope uses him only as one instance of a general vice. The great tableau which concludes the *First Dialogue* to the *Epilogue to the Satires* is a picture of the whole nation participating in the triumph of corruption, a picture of a social evil which the poet

---

[1] See Bolingbroke; *Of the Study and Use of History, Letter II*, 1752 ed., Vol. 2, p. 46.

presents with a new feeling for the satirist's responsibility
to his fellow men, and to truth and virtue:

> Lo, at the wheels of her triumphal car,
> Old England's Genius, rough with many a scar,
> Dragg'd in the dust, his arms hang idly round,
> His flag inverted trails along the ground.
> Our Youth all liveried o'er with foreign gold
> Before her dance, behind her crawl the old;
> See thronging millions to the Pagod run,
> And offer country, parent, wife or son,
> Hear her black trumpet thro' the Land proclaim
> That NOT TO BE CORRUPTED IS THE SHAME. . . .
> Yet may this verse (if such a verse remain)
> Show there was one who held it in disdain.[1]

The passion of Pope's satires is not simply the manly
rage of Oldham (which he condemned as Billingsgate),
nor the comic scorn of Dryden. It is the emotion of a poet
who feels himself bound by his duty to act as the historian
of his own times. In his Letters *Of the Study and Use of
History*, Bolingbroke, whose influence over Pope was immense, speaks of history as always appealing to our passions, to self-love, the delight in hearing what others or we
ourselves have done, and the pleasure men take in com-
memorating past actions. Pope recognized this same appeal
to the passions in poetry. 'In this impartial glass', he says,
speaking of his satire, he intends to expose 'myself, my
foes, my friends', to show the world to itself, in fact, as
history does. The taste of his age was ready for this; his
readers were willing to see the world reflected in its widest
sweep or in its local contemporary detail.

Pope's satire, even before he 'stoop'd to truth and
moralis'd his song', had been vivid and realistic in its

[1] Pope; *First Dialogue* to the *Epilogue to the Satires*, 11, 151–160 and 11, 171–172.

presentation of the social scene. The boudoir world of *The Rape of the Lock* is the hard brilliant scene of Restoration comedy warmed by sympathy and made more subtle and complex by irony. He had learned from Addison that there was such a thing as sympathetic realism as well as satiric realism, and that the two could be blended for a moral and witty purpose. Sheer delight in the visible world was one of Pope's peculiar attributes, but his age shared with him a taste for the descriptive and pictorial. Thomson's *Seasons*, with their expansive picturesque vistas of nature, and their vignettes of flowers and birds, were immediately popular. Topographical poems and landscape gardening showed how, in art and in life, men loved the visual pleasures of 'nature methodiz'd'. In art, history painting, like the epic in poetry, was considered the highest 'kind', but the eighteenth-century patron, whether he was a country gentleman or a successful merchant, preferred to commission a portrait or a conversation group which, while it pleased his eye, also reminded him of his own dignity and position. Similarly in literature, the love of realism was most firmly centred on men, their characters, their conduct, even their appearance.

Dryden himself had admired Ovid and Chaucer for their understanding of men and manners, and he explained the manners as 'the Passions, and in a larger sense the Descriptions of Persons and their very habits'.[1] Up to the end of the seventeenth century this interest in man in his local and everyday guise had been provided for by character studies like those in Earle's *Microcosmographie*, brief biographies, and the vivid biased portraits of contemporary figures with which the satirists enlivened their poems. For those who lived in London — and were not afraid of the disapproval of their more moral and prudent fellows — there

---

[1] Dryden; *Preface to the Fables*, 1700.

was the theatre, with its witty caricatured comic characters. But the appetite for literature describing man in a recognizable environment, in his dealings with his fellow men, had grown so strong at the beginning of the new century that this limited diet could no longer satisfy it. Addison again was one of the first to discover a way of giving fuller expression to this taste. The characters of Sir Roger de Coverley and his friends were more than *exempla* or illustrations of common types. They took part in a series of episodes which, like scenes from the drama, gave pleasure in themselves and seemed to make the figures of the protagonists more credible and lively. Readers of *The Spectator* papers grew as familiar with Sir Roger as with a personal acquaintance; he was not a character alone and isolated, but a man with an environment, a past and a present, a fully-conceived creation taking part in a life of his own. The germ of the new form of the novel lies in these essays.

Popular taste had always been curious about how people behaved, and had satisfied this curiosity with the life histories of highwaymen, thieves, and criminals, which were hawked about in broadsides after an execution, often with a crude message of moral exhortation attached to them. The writer who has the claim to be called our first novelist — Daniel Defoe — found a way of extending this sensational taste to the more literate, who before had contented themselves with those hot-house narratives of love and honour, the romances of authors like Mrs Aphra Behn. Defoe presented his fictions as if they were fact — true-life histories, personal confessions of robbers, prostitutes and kings' mistresses. The first-person narrative method, and the minute and accurate detail of his settings, whether these were exotic islands or the back streets of London, delighted readers who were beginning to realise the sheer pleasure of recognition in literature. These early novels,

Captain Jack, Moll Flanders, Roxana, Robinson Crusoe, were at once authentic and exciting, their characters credible, and their whole tone one of careful verisimilitude. They purported to be the actual experience of uncommon people who yet belonged to the common world.

The novel is the one great literary accession we owe to the eighteenth century. It is the only new form which the modern world has devised, and it is essentially the product of an age when public taste demanded an imitation of life which reflected its own habits and circumstances rather than ideal illustrations of essential qualities. Drama itself in the eighteenth century descended gradually from the rarefied heights of heroic tragedy to the domestic disasters of the *drame larmoyant*. But its appeal in contrast to that of the novel was limited indeed. When Richardson's two novels, *Pamela* and *Clarissa Harlowe*, appeared between 1740 and 1748, they sent literary Europe into raptures. The first concerns a servant girl and her triumphant if slightly ambiguous virtue. It shows how a good woman of inflexible principles can improve her position by prudence, and by a lively sense of her own worth, and of how to manage life and affairs. The second tells of a girl of good family, persecuted by her father and brother, and trapped by the intrigues of a young nobleman whose attitude to life comes straight out of Restoration comedy and the world of the wits. It is a heroic tragedy played out in contemporary society, with all the dignity and idealism of the older form, and all the detail and subtle realism of which the new form was capable.

Richardson wrote his 'great still books' for a public with the leisure to spend on extensive narratives, the pride in cultivated tastes which Addison had helped to inspire, and a healthy appetite for representations of everyday life dignified by the passion and the insight of art. Above all,

Richardson touched the hearts of his readers. 'This work is Nature', one epigrammatist said of *Clarissa*, while Young, the author of the celebrated *Night Thoughts*, wrote

> Nature, which favours to the few
> All art beyond imparts,
> To him presented at his birth
> The key of human hearts.

He was frequently compared with Shakespeare, for though Pope and Addison had set the passions on the side of truth, not since Shakespeare had anyone succeeded like Richardson in touching the springs of emotion, and displaying the subtleties of thought and action in common life. Richardson revealed to his delighted readers that there is no subject in literature so wide and profound as human relationships. His novels lack the supreme dignity of dramatic poetry; in its place they present us with the moving intimacy of prose realism.

Richardson's characters were still larger than life. The elements of the romance were lurking in his novels — the persecuted lady, the gentle perfect knight — but it is romance in daylight. Pamela broods lovingly over her velvet ribbons and round-eared cap bought from a pedlar; Clarissa heroically flaunts her virtue over a dish of tea as she confronts her ravisher; Sir Charles Grandison is firm on the social evil of duelling. These are rational and real creatures involved in extraordinary situations, and Richardson's passion for truth drove him to investigate the most unsuspected recesses of their personalities — the proud obstinacy of Clarissa, enamoured of her own virtue, the self-torment of Lovelace, and the irrepressible vitality of Pamela, the modest prude.

Eighteenth-century literature comes to maturity with Pope and Richardson. It is worldly literature which is yet moral; it is character literature which is yet exemplary and ideal. Above all it showed the world to itself in recognizable colours. Early novels were often taken for the truth. Mrs Thrale tells how an aunt of hers living in Preston was roused one morning by the ringing of the church bells, and her maid, 'bursting with joy', told her the cause: 'Why, madam, poor Pamela's married at last; the news came down to us in this morning's paper.'[1] Richardson would not have been displeased by this innocent credulity. But more sophisticated readers learned to appreciate the brilliant combination of formal contrivance and persuasive realism in Fielding's novels, or the subtle extravagances of Sterne, where the great literary conventions are lightly parodied, yet the power to move and the ability to create substantial characters never for a moment flags. The novel reflected the spirit of its age, and it presented to an eager public an image of the new ideal of the good man — the 'honnête homme', the hero of civil life; Parson Adams, that quixotic paragon of an everyday world, Tom Jones, the type of every honest natural young man, and my Uncle Toby, gentle, benevolent, eccentric but, in all his absurdities, instinct with human dignity.

By the 1740s the whole face of English literature had changed. The position of the professional author was very different from what it had been even at the beginning of the century. Pope's independence and the small fortune he had made by his translation of Homer could encourage a struggling author like Johnson, who himself succeeded by his own efforts and his own pen. The power of the purse in literary matters was passing from patrons to the booksellers during this period, and Johnson was glad of the change. With them a writer was dealing with his equals, and had no need of flattery, insincerity or solicita-

---

[1] *Thraliana*, ed. Balderstone, Oxford, 1942, Vol. I, p. 145.

tion. But Johnson had begun his career at a time when authorship was not yet entirely respectable, and he had suffered at first all the indignities and poverty of a hack journalist. A list of his early works gives some clue to the taste of his time. It includes translations and occasional poems, a life of Father Paul Sarpi, the Italian historian, a life of Boerhaave, lives of Admiral Blake, Sir Francis Drake and Philip Barretier, digests of parliamentary debates, and an essay 'On the Account of the Conduct of the Duchess of Marlborough' for the *Gentleman's Magazine*. The readers of this journal evidently liked their literature to be biographical and historical, and to have the odour of learning about it.

Though a young man might come up to London in 1740 with a satire in his pocket, as Johnson did, and make his way by reporting parliamentary debates and popularizing the lives of the great, in 1770 he was more likely to have a novel, or an improving and reflective poem, or a play to sell. Political pamphleteering was dying out as a branch of journalism because of the more efficient and highly-organized system of reporting party news in weekly journals and gazettes. Satire had inevitably grown more moral and more general; by the 1760s it was dying out. Churchill, the last satirist to recapture some of the old irreverence and fire, was rebuked by Johnson for using personal examples in his poems and thus securing a temporary *succès de scandale*. Public life was becoming more organized and less turbulent; public taste demanded more generally informative works, and more entertaining literature for its leisure hours. Goldsmith's numerous projects and hack works in the 1750s, as opposed to Johnson's a decade earlier, were lighter and more diverting. He offered the public *Memoirs of a Protestant condemn'd to the Gallies of France for his Religion*, a piece of sensationalism purporting to be true; an *Enquiry*

into the Present State of Polite Learning for dilettante critics;
The Bee, a series of 'essays on the most interesting subjects',
and a *Natural History* for amateur scientists.

Professional writers could no longer produce enough to
satisfy the public demand, and the century which saw the
establishment of the professional man of letters had not
run for fifty years before it hailed the return of the amateur.
He was a very different amateur, however, from the sage
or courtier of the past who had made writing his pastime.
In an essay in *The Adventurer*, 'The Itch of Writing Universal', Johnson remarks:

> the present age may be styled with great propriety the AGE
> OF AUTHORS; for perhaps there was never a time in which
> men of all degrees of ability, of every kind of education,
> of every profession and employment, were posting with
> ardour so general to the press.[1]

That confidence born of the general knowledge Addison
and his followers had so sedulously diffused, gave every man
the impression that he had something worth saying:

> The province of writing was formerly left to those who by
> study, or the appearance of study, were supposed to have
> gained knowledge unattainable to the busy part of mankind;
> but in these enlightened days, every man is qualified to
> instruct every other man; and he that beats the anvil or
> guides the plough, not contented with supplying corporal
> necessities, amuses himself in the hours of leisure with pro-
> viding intellectual pleasures for his countrymen.[2]

From being a craft of the highest dignity, the prerogative of the wise and great, literature in the eighteenth
century had become first a livelihood for the professional,
and finally a universal mode of self-expression. This last
development almost imperceptibly effected a change in

[1] *The Adventurer*, 1752–1754, no. 115.   [2] *Ibid.*

the tastes of readers and the style and subject matter of authors. It was a small step from writing about the external world in careful and authentic detail to writing about the mind of man, his inner springs of action and feeling, his thoughts 'that dodge conception to the very bourne of heaven'. The Romantic movement was the extraordinary culmination of that spirit of realism which first affected literature in the eighteenth century.

Johnson's ironic comment in *The Adventurer* summarizes one of the most lasting and significant aspects of the growth of literary taste in his age. Every period produces its writers; the eighteenth century raised up a race of readers, and saw the establishment of reading as the most universal pursuit and pastime of the educated man. One of the most remarkable evolutions of the age was the common taste for literature itself, for the pleasure and the profit of the written word.

IX

The Theatre and The Licensing Act of 1737

by PHYLLIS HARTNOLL

THE theatre in Great Britain today is under the control of the Crown, exercising its prerogative through one member of the Royal Household, the Lord Chamberlain, who alone has the right to license theatre buildings in London (with the exception of Drury Lane and Covent Garden) and plays for production in England, Scotland and Wales. His jurisdiction extends over all new plays, all plays written since 1843 which have not previously been licensed, and all new material written into old plays. He can also forbid the production of a play written before 1843 if he considers it advisable in the interests of public morality. If he refuses to issue a licence, there is no appeal from his decision. His veto is absolute. The only way to evade his authority is to form a theatre club and perform plays for members only, as is done at the Arts Theatre, the only permanent centre in London for the production of unlicensed plays. When one considers how much power is thus vested in one man, it is not surprising that the censorship is the subject of constant controversy, and that many people would like to see it abolished.

There has, of course, always been a certain amount of control over the theatre, but in earlier times it was exercised by different authorities in different ways. Actors came under the various statutes dealing with 'masterless men' which culminated in the 'Rogues, Vagabonds and

Sturdy Beggars' Act of 1572 (39 Eliz. c. 4), reinforced by the Vagrant Act of 1713 (12 Anne c. 23). It was one of the functions of the Master of the Revels, an official first mentioned in 1494, to ensure that plays contained no seditious or heretical matter, and in 1581 he was empowered to issue licences on payment of a fee for each performance. This was a form of censorship; but the duties of the Master of the Revels were light in comparison to the onerous burden laid on the Lord Chamberlain by the Licensing Act of 1737 (10 Geo. II c. 19) and confirmed by the Theatres Act of 1843 (6 & 7 Vict. c. 68) under which he still functions.

In order to understand the events which led to the passing of the Licensing Act, and so to the struggle against it which lasted well into the nineteenth century, it is necessary to go back to 1660. One of the first things Charles II did on his return to London was to arrange for the re-opening of the theatres, which had been closed since 1642. During that interval much of English stage tradition had been lost for ever. A fresh start had to be made, with new buildings and new companies of players, in which actresses figured for the first time. On May 15 Charles issued Letters Patent for the formation of two such companies to Thomas Killigrew and Sir William Davenant, who were both experienced men of the theatre, and had been staunch supporters of the Stuart cause and friends of the King in exile. Unfortunately these Patents were not limited to the lifetimes of the Patentees, nor was any arrangement made for their surrender. In this way Charles established, perhaps unwittingly, a monopoly in theatrical entertainment which was to be the cause of a fierce struggle for the next two hundred years, and whose repercussions are felt even today.

For about fifty years after the issue of the Patents, which still exist and are now in the possession of Drury Lane and

Covent Garden, making them independent of the Lord Chamberlain as licenser of buildings (though not as Censor), the evils of the monopoly were not too apparent. The first Patentees, though they may have been given their Patents for political reasons, were men of action and vision, with good companies and a good repertory. They, and their immediate successors, whether they held their rights by inheritance or by purchase, had no need to fear encroachments on their privileges. The theatre-going public of London was small, barely able to support two theatres, and there was no money to be made out of theatrical speculation. Such disputes as arose were among the actors and managers, and were largely ignored by the outside world. But the time was bound to come when the monopoly would be challenged, and in the early years of the eighteenth century several causes combined to bring the ensuing theatrical dissensions into the sphere of practical politics. The increase in population had brought about a corresponding increase in the number of potential playgoers, so that for the first time there was money to be made out of the theatre. At the same time events occurred which brought the Patents into disrepute, and permitted speculative managers to think themselves justified in setting up in opposition to the two Patent theatres.

It is unlikely that Charles II, in issuing the Patents, intended them to limit the Crown prerogative over public amusements, and neither he nor his successors considered themselves so limited. This was shown in 1709 when Queen Anne, on the advice of the Lord Chamberlain, ordered the closing of Drury Lane, which was in a state of chaos. At this time both Patents, by devious means, had fallen into the hands of an astute but rascally lawyer, Christopher Rich, who seems to have been the only person to realize their potential value. He used his powers tyrannically, and the actors appealed to the Lord Chamberlain for redress. Rich, however, chose to ignore the orders given him in respect of salaries and other matters, relying on the immunity conferred on him by the Patents. The Lord Chamberlain's resentment at his behaviour was reinforced by the complaints of a Colonel Brett, one of the Patentees forced out by Rich's manoeuvres. He had influence at Court, and his remonstrances, combined with those of the Lord Chamberlain, led Queen Anne not only to close Drury Lane, but to confer a licence for its re-opening on one William Collier, a Member of Parliament who held a small share in one Patent.

This intervention by the Crown in theatrical matters was again apparent in 1714, when George I issued a licence to Sir Richard Steele, only to revoke it five years later on the complaint of the Lord Chamberlain. Steele fought a protracted legal battle, claiming that his Patent ranked equally with those issued by Charles II, but the influence of the Lord Chamberlain was too strong, and Steele's company of actors was disbanded.

During all these troubles Rich had held on to the original Patents, and he passed them on to his son John, England's first Harlequin. One remained in force for Drury Lane, but under the other John Rich opened the Lincoln's Inn Fields theatre in 1714, transferring it to Covent Garden in 1731.

All this juggling with the Patents, their use as social and political weapons, and the uncertainty about the extent of the powers they conferred, combined to encourage the activities of those who chose to ignore them. A general contempt for a monopoly sanctioned by time but not firmly established in law went hand in hand with a desire to profit by the large number of playgoers who were dissatisfied with the entertainment provided by the Patent theatres. This led to the opening of a number of unlicensed playhouses which, not wishing to trespass too openly upon the 'legitimate'[1] drama, contented themselves with mixed entertainments, farces and burlesques. But a natural desire to attract and hold the attention of their audiences led to an increased dependence on topical sketches, and so satire came into the playhouse. The political troubles of the early eighteenth century had already stimulated the output of satiric writers in journals and pamphlets, and it was only a matter of time before they made use of the new medium offered them by the unlicensed theatres. Satire is very much at home in the theatre, where it makes an immediate appeal due to the intimacy between actor and audience. It can also be more effective than a pamphlet, for instance, because it reinforces the satirical word by caricature of voice, gesture, personal idiosyncrasies and even peculiarities of costume; and in a largely illiterate age it quickly reached a wider audience and was easily disseminated by gossip. In addition it suited the requirements of an unlicensed playhouse, as in the event of trouble the actors could blame the author, the author the actors, and the manager anyone but himself. Political satire still flourishes in the Continental theatre, but it has almost disappeared from the London stage, thanks to the vigilance of the Lord Chamberlain — an ironic end for a *genre* which contributed more than anything else to the passing of the Act which gave him his present powers.[2]

As the battle for the stage was to be fought on political ground, it might perhaps be a good thing to survey the

[1] The term 'legitimate' covered the plays of Shakespeare and his contemporaries, those of the Restoration, and all new plays, particularly tragedies, which contained no singing or dancing. The monopoly was always taken as referring to legitimate drama only.

[2] Debarred from the stage, the vigour of the political satire seems to have taken refuge in the political cartoon, which has for so long directed a fierce and searching light upon all great figures in public life.—Ed.

scene. George II had come to the throne in 1727. In some respects an admirable person — he could at least, unlike his father, speak English — he nevertheless left much of the business of ruling England to his wife, Queen Caroline, who was assisted by the first minister (the term Prime Minister was not then in use), Sir Robert Walpole. Walpole was undoubtedly the outstanding political figure of his day. A man of robust common sense, practical, jovial, coarse, a heavy drinker and a great foxhunter, he had no time for religion, reformers, or the arts. He certainly had no love for the theatre. The best one can say of him is that he hated war, and bent most of his energies to the preservation of peace for England. A man of great ability, he had a penetrating insight into the weaknesses of his fellow-creatures, and believed that most men can be bought if you know what price to offer. Acting on this belief, he practised bribery and corruption, mainly in an indirect way, by awarding positions and pensions to those who would support him. In this he was only following the custom of the time, when few men would work for or against the Government without hope of reward.

The Lord Chamberlain at this time, Thomas Pelham-Holles, Duke of Newcastle, was one of Walpole's adherents, a staunch, though somewhat eccentric, party politician. Also on the Government side was Lord Hervey, author of the *Memoirs of the Reign of George II*. The Opposition was led ostensibly by William Pulteney, with the assistance of Sir William Wyndham, but in reality by Bolingbroke, who, though still debarred from taking part in public life, had returned from exile in 1725, and was very busy behind the scenes.

From the satirist's point of view there was very little to choose between the Government and the Opposition, and unless they were handsomely rewarded for writing on one side or the other, they lashed out impartially at both. The main charges against Walpole were that he ruled by bribery, practised nepotism, was tyrannic, perfidious, jealous of the ability of others, the betrayer of his country at home and abroad, and that he was immoral in his private life and had accumulated a vast fortune at the public expense. For the purposes of dramatic satire it was not necessary that these charges — and the many similar ones levelled at the Opposition — should be true, but only that audiences should be willing to believe them. And this they were very ready to do, provided they were presented with some semblance of wit and a certain amount of music and spectacle, as they certainly were in John Gay's *The Beggar's Opera*.

This, the first ballad-opera, was put on at Lincoln's Inn Fields by John Rich on January 29, 1728 N.S.,[1] after it had been refused by Colley Cibber for Drury Lane. It has been revived several times in recent years, and appears to be nothing more than a harmless gibe at the expense of highwaymen and their unlawful frolics. On its first production it had a political significance which it has now lost. Homes Dudden, in his life of Fielding, says: 'Everyone enjoyed the allusions . . . to Sir Robert's rough manners and convivial habits, to his break with Townshend... and to his delicate domestic situation between Lady Walpole and Miss Skerrett' (an allusion to Macheath's song 'How happy could I be with either'). Since Walpole was known ironically as the Great Man, they enjoyed too Peachum's remark: 'But really, my dear, it grieves one's heart to take off a great man. When I consider . . . how much we have already got by him, and how much more we may get;

[1] Until 1752 the civil and legal year began on March 25, and the earlier months therefore belonged to the preceding year. This is referred to as Old Style (O.S.), and dates brought into conformity with modern usage as New Style (N.S.). All the dates in this essay are N.S.

methinks I can't find it in my heart to have a hand in his death.' And no one had any difficulty in recognizing 'Robin Bagshot . . . alias Bluff Bob . . . alias Bob Booty'. The piece was a great success, and had the unprecedented run, for those days, of sixty-two performances. The wits said it had made 'Gay rich, and Rich gay'. But the official newspaper, *The Craftsman* (No. 85), was less amused, and went so far as to call it 'the most venomous allegorical libel against the Government that has appeared for many years'. A somewhat similar reaction was aroused in the 1930s by Bertolt Brecht's modernized version of Gay's ballad-opera as *Die Dreigroschen-Oper* (*The Threepenny Opera*), with music by Kurt Weill, which has, incidentally, been running in New York, where political satire is a vital element of the theatrical scene, for the last five years.

Plays at this time were not licensed before production, but the Lord Chamberlain, who had taken over some of the functions of the Master of the Revels, could suppress them, either during rehearsal or after the first night, without giving his reasons. As Homes Dudden remarks: 'There seems to have been very little method, and still less justice, in the procedure of the Censor at this period.' After the success of *The Beggar's Opera* its sequel, *Polly*, was forbidden, as were several other plays, mainly on political grounds. The Patent Theatres, warned that the Lord Chamberlain was on the alert, reverted to less dangerous topics, and left satire for the time being to the unlicensed playhouses, who were not slow to seize their opportunity. As booths and small theatres multiplied, so they came to rely more and more on contemporary satire to establish themselves and draw in their audiences.

In the struggle which was now developing between the Patentees and the unlicensed managers on the one hand, and the Government and the theatre on the other, the two

most important unlicensed playhouses were the Little
Theatre in the Hay, and Goodman's Fields Theatre in
Ayliffe Street, Whitechapel. The latter does not come into
the story until much later, and can for the moment be
disregarded. The Little Theatre in the Hay, the ancestor
of the present Haymarket, was built in 1720 by John
Potter, a carpenter, who hoped to make money by letting
it out for musical and theatrical entertainments, particularly to foreign companies visiting London. In fact,
as Sybil Rosenfeld points out in her *Foreign Theatrical
Companies in Great Britain*, the first actors to hire it were
French. Other attractions seen there were concerts, acrobats, dancers, burlesques and farces. These last soon developed a satirical content, and on March 29, 1729, there
was acted at the Haymarket a wild jumble of farcical
incidents entitled *Hurlothrumbo; or, the Supernatural*, which
achieved almost as great a success as *The Beggar's Opera*.
The author, Samuel Johnson — not the great lexicographer
and friend of Boswell, but a native of Cheshire — played
the chief part himself. He was undoubtedly mad, but his
madness had a touch of genius, and his dialogue, for all its
incoherence, contained some strokes of wit, and many
telling reflections on the follies of great men. The political
references, which are practically unintelligible now, were
readily understood, and helped to give the play its contemporary notoriety.

It was not only in the playhouses that satire found a
home. It appeared also in the small portable booths set up,
like Punch and Judy shows, at the corners of the streets. In
1730, in a booth belonging to the travelling showman
Penkethman, there was acted a droll, or short play, entitled *Wat Tyler or Jack Straw*, which openly denounced
the corruption and inefficiency of Walpole's administration. The time was coming when the authorities would

have to take notice of such flagrant violations of the law. As Watson Nicholson says in his account of this period, *The Struggle for a Free Stage in London*: 'The condition into which the stage was rapidly drifting could not long continue without a crisis. The climax to be reached needed only a master in satire.' And such a master inevitably appeared, in the person of Henry Fielding.

Fielding, better known nowadays as a novelist, was for many years an outstanding figure in the theatre, and it was to his activities, more than to anything else, that his contemporaries attributed the passing of the Licensing Act. When he wrote his first play, at the age of nineteen, dramatic literature was in a bad way. The bawdy vitality of Restoration comedy had given way to sentimentality; pseudo-classicism had replaced tragedy. There were too many counter-attractions — Italian opera, ballad-opera, farce, pantomime[1] — all spectacular and scenic, and making full use of song and dance, for the serious drama to flourish. But they provided a perfect medium for satire.

Fielding's first three plays contain practically no political satire at all, though some may have been read into them by the audience. *Love in Several Masques* (1728) was a comedy of intrigue aimed at the effeminate fop of the day; *The Temple Beau* (1729) satirizes the wild young man-about-town; *The Author's Farce* (1730), the first of Fielding's plays to be done at the Haymarket, satirizes society in the persons of the rapacious landlady, the penniless poet and the rascally bookseller, and the theatre in the persons of two stupid managers, intended to represent the Drury Lane Patentees, Colley Cibber and Robert Wilks.

It is difficult to be sure how much political satire Field-

---

[1] This is not the modern pantomime, traditionally associated with Christmas, but a wordless mime play, derived from the Italian *commedia dell' arte*, in which Harlequin was always the chief character.

ing intended to introduce into his next play, *Tom Thumb the Great*, which is mainly a burlesque of heroic tragedy. Given Walpole's nickname, the audience would be bound to look for resemblances to him in a character surnamed 'the Great', and they no doubt found them. But the satire was not keen enough to alarm the authorities, and when the play was later expanded from a two-act afterpiece to a three-act comedy, under the title of *The Tragedy of Tragedies; or, the Life and Death of Tom Thumb the Great*, the literary satire was more apparent than the political.

It was with *The Welsh Opera; or, the Grey Mare the Better Horse* that Fielding came out boldly into the political arena. This ballad-opera, first seen at the Haymarket in April, 1731, was an attack on both political parties which also brought the Royal Family upon the stage. The chief characters are two servants in a Welsh household, Robin the Butler and William the Coachman, whose quarrels reflect those of Walpole and Pulteney. Their master and mistress are thinly-veiled (but not unpleasing) portraits of George II and Queen Caroline. The King is represented as 'the best of landlords', but one who prefers to leave the management of his estate to his wife — 'Let her govern, while I smoke.' Their son, Owen, represents the unfortunate Frederick, Prince of Wales, and Robin's allies in his skirmishes with William are John the Groom (Hervey) and Thomas the Gardener (Newcastle). The plot, which is very slight, tells how Owen, by means of forged letters, gets Robin to believe that his sweetheart is playing him false with William, and it is merely a peg on which to hang outspoken topical comments directed at most of the well-known politicians of the day. Robin (Walpole) comes off worst; but William (Pulteney) is really no better, and is shown making trouble for Robin in the hope of getting his place.

This highly topical play is not perhaps important as dramatic literature, but it certainly packed a very considerable political punch, and Fielding, elated at its success, withdrew it, extended it to three acts, and renamed it *The Grub-Street Opera*, in allusion to the hack writers of abusive political pamphlets.[1] But the new version was not destined to be acted, though it was published. Either the actors took fright, or Fielding, acting on a strong hint from the Lord Chamberlain, prompted no doubt by Walpole, decided he had gone far enough. The Haymarket reverted to such harmless diversions as rope-dancing, acrobats and French players, while Fielding, having made his peace with Drury Lane, produced there five plays which dealt light-heartedly with the social scene.

He might not have meddled with politics again, had it not been for the repercussions of the hated Excise Bill of 1733 (which Walpole dropped), and the temptation offered by the announcement of a parliamentary election. The opportunity was too good to be missed, and into a ballad-opera entitled *Don Quixote in England* Fielding put three election-scenes, satirizing the conduct of candidates and electors. It is essential, one character declares, that there should be a contested election, otherwise there will be no money for the Mayor, the townspeople, the voters and the publicans. When no second candidate presents himself, the Mayor persuades Don Quixote to stand. This gives Fielding the chance to get in several shrewd knocks at contemporary election malpractices, particularly bribery; and in view of the allegation made against Walpole that he had enriched himself at the public expense, no one could fail to miss the significance of Don Quixote's remark: 'I'll

[1] Grub Street, according to Dr Johnson, was 'a small street . . . much inhabited by writers of small histories, dictionaries and temporary poems'; the term was later extended to cover all hack-work, particularly of an offensive type.

act like other wise governors, fall to plundering as fast as I can, and when I have made my fortune, why, let them turn me out if they will.'

This new play was rather surprisingly accepted by Drury Lane, but it got crowded out of the repertory by the success of a pantomime featuring a Dutch giant, and not wishing to miss the moment when it would be most effective, Fielding took it to the Haymarket. It was performed in mid-April, 1734, and published on the very day on which the writs for the election were issued. There were great hopes, on the part of the anti-Walpole faction, that he would be defeated at the polls, but in the event he was returned with a comfortable, though reduced, majority. For some reason this seems to have decided Fielding to throw in his lot with the Opposition. Perhaps he was influenced by the presence in the new House of Commons of two old school-friends, William Pitt and George Lyttelton, and by the overtures made to him by Chesterfield, who had been quick to realize the value to his party of such a satiric pen. Whatever the reason, he now took the bold step of going into management at the Haymarket, where he put on his two most audacious political satires — *Pasquin*[1] and *The Historical Register for the Year 1736*.

Pasquin, produced on March 5, 1736, was cast in the form of a rehearsal of a play called *The Election*. Its satire on corrupt practices indulged in by candidates during an election is much sharper and more bitter than that in *Don Quixote in England*. It was a great success, almost as great a success as *The Beggar's Opera*, and for the same reasons. Politics, of course, was only one of Fielding's targets, and it may be that he did not set out deliberately to satirize

[1] The term 'pasquinade' was applied at this time to lampoons and satirical writings. It came from the name (originally that of a sharp-tongued cobbler) of a statue in Rome on which it was the custom to hang satirical verses on St Mark's Day.

the political scene. He took his material where he found it, and that was a vulnerable spot.

Fielding was now getting into his stride. In his capacity as manager of the Haymarket, he was responsible for the appearance of several new plays which were aimed at the Government. One was an anonymous farce which laid great stress on the fact that Walpole, a heavy drinker, was known to have supported the recent severe tax on spirits; in another he was satirized as Macplunderkan, King of Roguemania. There can be no doubt that Walpole was Fielding's chief target, but in fairness to him, and to his fellow-satirists, it must be said that they were not far off the mark. The report of the Select Commission appointed by the Government to investigate the criticisms contained in the satires revealed that they were not exaggerated. However admirable Walpole's ends, his means were sometimes open to question, and he certainly gave many handles to his enemies.

In March, 1737, Fielding brought out the last and most brilliant of his political satires, *The Historical Register for the Year 1736*. It was customary at this time to publish annually a summary of all the important events of the past twelve months. In imitation of this Fielding strung together a series of six episodes purporting to deal with the events of 1736. Cast once again in the form of a rehearsal, like *Pasquin*, this sequence contained two theatrical scenes, two social, and two political.

The first political scene shows five politicians in council. As they leave the stage, an observer, in answer to a question, says: 'They have finished the business they met about, which was to agree on a tax; that being done, they are gone to raise it.' In the second scene Fielding has in view those members of the Opposition who had been bribed to desert their party. He points out that they are then used to swell the vote in favour of heavier taxation, by which means the Government was able to recover the money spent in bribing them. These scenes are openly hostile to Walpole, but even in the theatrical scenes Fielding seems to have been unable to resist a dig at him. A manager (intended to represent Cibber) is seen handing out parts, 'as a politician hands out preferments', and then insisting that the actors must do only what he tells them. He also says of the public, when told they will hiss his play: 'Let them hiss, so long as we get their money. There, Sir, you have the sentiment of a Great Man.' In the afterpiece to *The Historical Register*, a short farce on the subject of Orpheus and Eurydice, Walpole figures again as Mr Pillage, a manager determined to foist his play on the public, as, it was currently asserted, Walpole forced his unpopular policy on the country by bribing the members of Parliament. In a final scene of what would nowadays be called 'wishful thinking' Mr Pillage is shown, deserted by his friends, his play damned, drinking himself into a stupor.

Even without the cumulative effect of the smaller pieces, the satire in *Pasquin* and *The Historical Register* was too blatant to be overlooked, and there were many who thought that Fielding had over-reached himself. On May 7, 1737, the official newspaper, *The Daily Gazetteer*, warned him of possible repressive measures, to which he replied by publishing his two offending plays with an introduction. Starting off mildly enough with a tirade against theatrical abuses, he develops his theme into an attack on political mismanagement, and announces that 'while we have any liberty left among us' he will continue to ridicule 'vice and imposture'. In a letter to the Opposition paper, *Common Sense*, for May 21, signed Pasquin, and almost certainly by Fielding, he said that 'ridicule had always been a weapon against corruption', and that criticism of the Government was as permissible on the stage as in a pamphlet or news-paper.

He had perhaps forgotten that ridicule on the stage is more wounding and less easy to refute than that on the printed page. He certainly seems to have forgotten that his theatre was wide open to attack. He should have been warned that its comparative freedom had already been threatened twice in recent years, once in 1733, when a bill 'to regulate the playhouses', strongly backed by Walpole, was debated for two hours, but did not come to a division, and again in 1735, when a similar bill, introduced by Sir John Barnard, was withdrawn only because one clause was thought to give too much power to the Lord Chamber-lain — an ironic conclusion, in view of the fact that the Licensing Act was soon to give him even greater powers.

These two abortive attempts to bring in theatrical legisla-tion showed which way the wind was blowing. Two factors were operating in favour of greater severity. Politicians on the whole take themselves seriously, and are averse to being made to look ridiculous even in historical, mythological or imaginary guise; and there is no more potent weapon than ridicule in the hands of a man who knows his job, as London had now discovered. And while the politicians were smarting under the blows of a shrewd satirist, the Patentees saw their audiences drawn off, themselves and their productions parodied, and their cherished monopoly in danger. In their efforts to beat the unlicensed theatres at their own game, the egregious Cibber was slaughtering Shakespeare at Drury Lane, while Rich's whole energies were given to pantomime, at which he excelled. Good writers, disgusted at the conditions which prevailed in the Patent theatres, refused to work for them. And since the unlicensed theatres could not, and the Patent theatres would not, put on serious drama, there was nowhere for it to take refuge. Something had to be done. This might have been the propitious moment for the founding of a National Theatre. Indeed, several plans were put forward for a so-called Third Theatre, but between the greed of the Patentees and the repressive inertia of the Lord Chamberlain, they came to nothing.

The Government was anxious enough to bring in new legislation to regulate the theatres; all it needed was a good pretext for doing so. One came in a most unexpected way, indirectly, too, for its first appearance had nothing to do with the stage. The Opposition newspaper, *Common Sense*, emboldened perhaps by the prevailing spirit of licence, published in March, 1737, a satire on Walpole's administration called 'The Vision of the Golden Rump'. This describes the rites practised before an imaginary Indian idol, who had a wooden head and a rump of gold. There is an echo in the title of the Biblical account of the worship of the Golden Calf in Exodus, and perhaps an allusion to the so-called Rump Parliament of 1648. The article was the inspiration behind a print,[1] brought out hurriedly in the same month and widely circulated, entitled 'The Festival of the Golden Rump' which showed a priest (obviously Walpole) leading the people in prayer before the idol. Here, if only it had been theatrical, was satire too vicious, too obscene, to be ignored; and by a curious chance, which has never been explained, and about which various theories are current, the Golden Rump found its way into the theatre, and gave Walpole just the pretext he needed for coming down heavily on his enemies, particularly Fielding.

Oddly enough, it was not from the Haymarket that provocation came, but from Goodman's Fields Theatre,

[1] There is a copy of it in the British Museum Print Room: *Political and Social Satires*, No. 2327.

where Henry Giffard, an adventurous and experienced Irish actor, had been operating successfully for several years. Like the other unlicensed managers, he relied mainly on entertainments of song and spectacle, burlesque, farce and satire. In May, 1737, at the height of the scandal over the Golden Rump, Giffard received the manuscript of an anonymous two-act farce, apparently based on the article in *Common Sense*, and full of the most scurrilous attacks on Walpole and his ministers. He immediately took it to Walpole, who gave him £1,000 for it (and no doubt considered it cheap at the price), communicated the worst passages to the King and Parliament, and used them as an excuse for putting through the famous Licensing Act, in the form of an amendment to the Vagrant Act of 1731. The new Act re-established, far more stringently this time, the monopoly created by Charles II, and brought all plays under the censorship of the Lord Chamberlain, a regularized and strictly-enforced censorship which still exists, though it is relaxed from time to time by re-adjustments which mitigate its severity. It was by virtue of this Act that licences were refused for plays by Ibsen, Shaw, and, more recently, Beckett and Tennessee Williams.

The rapidity with which the Licensing Act was put through can be judged by the fact that it was introduced into the House on May 24, at a time when many Members had already left for the country, and received the Royal Assent on June 21. Both Pulteney and Chesterfield spoke against it, the latter most eloquently, saying that it was intended, not to regulate the playhouses, but to silence inconvenient criticism of the Government, and that it was an encroachment not only upon liberty, but upon property: 'Wit . . . is a sort of property; it is the property of those who have it, and too often the only property they have to depend on. . . . I plead the cause of wit; I plead the cause of the British stage.' But his pleas were of no avail against the resentment of Walpole and the indifference of the other Members present, and the bill went through.

There are several puzzling features about this episode. First, we may ask, how did Walpole manage to put through such an important piece of legislation so quickly and so quietly? Even allowing for the apathy and reduced membership of the House, why was there so little agitation outside? The Act must have been hotly debated during that month of May 24 to June 21. In fact, we are told by the Abbé Le Blanc, then visiting London, that 'it occasioned a universal murmur in the nation, and was openly complained of in the public papers; in all the coffee-houses of London it was treated as an unjust law, and manifestly contrary to the liberties of the people of England'.[1] Yet on investigation[2] there appears to be very little comment on it in the newspapers — perhaps Walpole muzzled the Press? — nor is it much mentioned in the letters and diaries of the period. One would have expected Pitt and Lyttelton to protest against legislation aimed so openly at their old school-friend. Had Fielding so alienated the Opposition, as well as the Government, that they kept quiet, knowing he would be the chief sufferer? It seems certain that the Patentees must have had a hand in the affair, or why were the Patents so strongly reinforced? Certainly the success of Fielding's work, in a small theatre, with poor actors, had shown up the folly and incompetence of Drury Lane and Covent Garden. This may have been their revenge.

Secondly, we may ask, why did Giffard, who had already

[1] See the note by Lowe in Vol. I of his edition of *An Apology for the Life of Colley Cibber*, p. 278.

[2] For confirmation of this opinion I am indebted to Professor Emmett L. Avery of Washington State University, editor of Part II of *The London Stage, 1660–1800*.

put himself in jeopardy by running an unlicensed theatre, and staging productions which attacked the Government, take the manuscript of *The Golden Rump* to the one man it was most likely to offend? Had he been given a hint that such a move would be well rewarded? Certainly £1,000 was a lot of money for such a simple action, but did he hope also to get a licence for Goodman's Fields? or to bring about the closing of the Haymarket?

Who, finally, was the author of this play which came so conveniently upon its hour? The manuscript seems to have disappeared. All we know of it is from hearsay, and from some garbled extracts. Horace Walpole, finding these latter among his father's papers, attributed the piece to Fielding. But this seems unlikely. Fielding had enough material of his own without raking over someone else's unsavoury messes, and if he had written it, he would surely have put it on at his own theatre. Nor is it likely that he sent it to Goodman's Fields, hoping Giffard would put it on, and so get into trouble. Whatever his faults, he was not vindictive. And nothing we know of the play seems to fit with our knowledge of Fielding's work.

It is almost equally unlikely that Walpole himself wrote the play, as was suggested in an article in the *Town and Country Magazine*, Oct., 1787. Why should he, when there were plenty of people to do it for him? — John Henley, for instance, the parson-buffoon, whom Walpole had previously engaged to write in support of the Ministry in *The Hyp Doctor*: Thomas Pitt (the Mother Osborne of Pope's *Dunciad*), whom Walpole had made editor of *The Daily Gazetteer*: Mrs Eliza Haywood, the 'scribbling woman', who wrote scandalous novels about contemporary figures thinly disguised as fiction. Once the Government had seen — and it was not difficult to see — how the scandal of the Golden Rump could be used against the stage, it would be simple enough to find someone who could recast it as a play. Unless and until the script, or some portions of it, are recovered, we cannot begin to guess who wrote it. And until we know that, Walpole must lie under grave suspicion of having acted as *agent provocateur* in this matter, and Giffard of having been suborned to assist him. How true Walpole must have thought his dictum that every man has his price when Giffard betrayed the theatre for £1,000!

Immediately on the passing of the Licensing Act all the unlicensed playhouses were closed, and the actors and managers were out of work. But the blow fell heaviest on Fielding, as had no doubt been intended. He lost his theatre, and he could not expect the Censor to license, or the Patentees to perform, anything written by him. Wisely, having a wife and family to support, he gave up playwriting, except for a few trifles of no account, and turned to fiction. Perhaps it should be laid to the credit of the Licensing Act that it was indirectly responsible for *Tom Jones* and *Joseph Andrews*!

For the next hundred years the Patentees were to fight a losing battle to retain their monopoly, and enterprising managers were to spend their energies trying to outwit the Lord Chamberlain. To get round the clause 'no person . . . shall act . . . for gain hire or reward' tickets were sold for concerts, for auctions, for a 'Dish of Tea' or Chocolate, and a play given free of charge. Playgoers were invited to assist at students' rehearsals, demonstrations, exercises or inventions. Several attempts were made to resolve the difficulties caused by the Licensing Act. The Interlude Bill of 1788 might have regularized the situation of the unlicensed theatres to everyone's satisfaction, but it was defeated on its second reading by the combined efforts of Fox and Sheridan. The latter was in a strong position, being both a

Member of Parliament and a Patent holder at Drury Lane. It was to his advantage to defeat all efforts to straighten out the chaotic conditions which are so admirably summed up by Watson Nicholson:

> Thus legislation stood, respecting the theatres, at the close of the eighteenth century: The Lord Chamberlain was chief authority in Westminster, the home of the Patent Theatres; magistrates in London, and within twenty miles thereof, might license certain species of theatrical amusements; magistrates outside the twenty-mile circle could authorise the regular drama for a limited period each year; while special legislation in the case of individual cities [among them Bath, Birmingham, Bristol, Manchester, Edinburgh] permitted the same privileges as those enjoyed by the two Patent Houses. . . . No more complicated or cumbrous legislation could be imagined.

All these shifts and expedients were due to the efforts of the Patentees to retain their monopoly. Though public and informed opinion had already come to the conclusion that this was no longer possible, or indeed desirable, it took nearly fifty years of hard work on the part of the reformers to break the stranglehold of Drury Lane and Covent Garden, and in doing so they were forced to retain the censorship. In their efforts at ending the monopoly they were greatly assisted by two enlightened Lords Chamberlain, Lord Dartmouth and Lord Conyngham. By 1843 everyone knew that the monopoly created by Charles II in 1660 was dead. The Theatres Act of that year merely recorded its demise.

X

Foreign Impressions of England in the Eighteenth Century

by W. D. ROBSON-SCOTT

'To see oursels as others see us' is no doubt a salutary experience, both individually and nationally; it is also a useful way of supplementing the more usual channels of historical evidence. What the casual visitor to these shores may lack in knowledge and accuracy is outweighed by the freshness of his observation. The foreigner will note many a point, just because it differs from conditions in his own country, which the native would pass unregarded. As late as 1782, for instance, a German tourist remarks on the absence of walled towns in England compared with his fatherland, where the fortified town is still the rule, behind which observation lies a whole vista of English history.

This source of information is particularly valuable for the period under review, for in the early decades of the eighteenth century a marked improvement becomes noticeable in the quality of foreign accounts of England. Before this time such documents had been mainly topographical; the national character and its reflection in the customs and institutions of the country were for the most part disregarded. Now, about 1730, all this is changed; there is a sharp shift from the topographical to the sociological. The peculiarities of the English character and of English forms of government and social life become of absorbing interest to our visitors.

This transformation was brought about largely through certain French and Swiss visitors of distinction who came to this island in the early decades of the century. The most influential, though not the first, of these was Voltaire, whose *Letters concerning the English Nation* (1733) did much to reveal English civilization to the Continent.

It is difficult for us now to realize how little the achievements of English civilization were known abroad at this period. Despite Elizabethan literature and music, despite the Royal Society and Locke and Newton, England still counted for little as a cultural factor beyond these shores. The essential significance of Voltaire's *Letters* lay in the fact that a man of his reputation ventured to take English civilization seriously, and to consider it worthy to rank with the long-accepted civilizations of France and Italy. This involved a complete reorientation in the Continental attitude towards this country, a reorientation which we soon find reflected in the accounts of foreign visitors.

Voltaire is not interested in topographical data; earlier writers had already dealt adequately with this aspect of the subject. Nor is he interested in the English character as such. His *Letters* are concerned with the religious and political systems and with the literary and scientific achievements of the nation. Above all, they are concerned with the idea of freedom. When Voltaire visited England in the spring of 1726 he came as a fugitive from tyranny, so it was natural that this aspect of English life should have impressed him beyond all else; natural, too, that his picture of England and the English should have been coloured by his desire to point the contrast between the virtues of England and the shortcomings of his native country in this respect. Liberty is the keynote of the book, liberty in religion, in politics, in the arts and sciences.

Voltaire begins by describing the variety of religious

sects, which is itself a proof of English liberty. 'England is properly the country of sectarists. An Englishman, as one to whom liberty is natural, may go to heaven his own way.' Moreover, this multiplicity of sects has its practical uses. 'If one religion only were allowed in England, the government would very possibly become arbitrary; if there were but two, the people would cut one another's throats; but as there are such a multitude, they all live happy and in peace.' Similarly in the political sphere: 'The English are the only people upon earth who have been able to prescribe limits to the power of kings by resisting them; and who, by a series of struggles, have at last established that wise government, where the prince is all-powerful to do good, and at the same time is restrained from committing ill; where the nobles are great without insolence, though there are no vassals; and where the people share in the government without confusion.' The same holds good in intellectual matters. It is because such great philosophers and scientists as Bacon, Locke or Newton have been able to pursue their studies and researches with untrammelled freedom that their achievements have been so remarkable.

It is true that in the field of literature the same principle does not obtain. Here liberty is apt to be confused with licence. Thus the English tragedies are utterly lacking in order and propriety, though one cannot deny them flashes of genius. Shakespeare, for instance, 'boasted a strong, fruitful genius, but had not so much as a single spark of Good Taste, or knew one rule of the drama.' Nevertheless his 'monstrous farces, to which the name of tragedy is given', have individual passages 'so beautiful, so noble and so dreadful' that they succeed marvellously on the English stage. This may not sound very high praise, but to a Europe ignorant of the very name of Shakespeare it was in the nature of a revelation. It may be said without exaggeration that these few remarks in Voltaire's *Letter on Tragedy* first introduced the greatest of English poets to Europe and the world.

However hesitating his commendation of Shakespeare, Voltaire felt strong approval for other aspects of our literature. He thinks more highly of our comedies than our tragedies, and he has warm praise for the satires of Rochester, Butler's *Hudibras*, Swift, and above all Pope. Moreover the English not only have great writers, philosophers and scientists, but they know how to honour them, by rewarding them with emoluments in their life and by showing them due reverence after their death, as witness the tombs of Newton and other men of genius in Westminster Abbey.

The contemporary reader of Voltaire's *Letters* would take away with him above all else the impression of England as a land of liberty and enlightenment, where science, philosophy and the arts flourished under a wise and tolerant system of government. In this they set the tone for the great majority of visitors to this country, at least up to the time of the French Revolution.

After Voltaire the most influential foreign observations on the English in the early eighteenth century come from Béat Louis de Muralt, a native of Berne, whose *Lettres sur les Anglois* were first published in 1725, though they refer to a visit he made to this country in 1694. Muralt's letters form a useful complement to Voltaire's, for they are primarily concerned with the national character as such. He sees the essence of this character to lie in two related qualities: common sense and independence of mind. The English, he finds, pay little attention to the opinions of others and even dare to pass for fools if need be, which is after all a great step towards wisdom. They are less obsequious to the great than other nations (he is thinking particularly of the France of Louis XIV), and are not afraid to utter unpalatable truths when this is called for. Hence 'it is desirable that there should be enough Englishmen scattered throughout the world to tell the people the truths that no one else dares to impart' — a sound if unusual argument for the British Empire!

In this mental independence Muralt sees their true claim to courage. They are not a military nation, and do not make much of military distinctions, but they excel in 'that true courage, for lack of which the other kinds have been introduced among men: I mean the courage to do bravely a good deed, and to dare to follow reason against custom.'

Of course they have their weaknesses, and one of these is what Muralt calls 'un petit reste de férocité', exemplified, for instance, by the violent sports so beloved of the populace, and even more by the callous indifference of the English in the face of death. Though common sense is their prevailing characteristic, once the English do depart from it, they fall easily into extremes of eccentricity. They are indeed a nation of extremes, both in good and bad, and they are not less a mass of contradictions, which, he adds, is only to say that they are after all human.

It will be seen that Muralt's attitude to the English is predominantly friendly, but it is not uncritical. He has a good deal to say of their immorality, but their chief fault is laziness, both physical and mental. To their mental laziness he attributes their astonishing indifference to the evil conditions around them; for instance, in the matter of the debtors' prisons, where the unfortunate victims are forced to nourish themselves, and, if they cannot do so, die of starvation. 'The great cruelty of the English consists in permitting evil rather than in committing it.' And finally, though he defends them against the customary accusation of arrogance to foreigners, he has to admit that they have an overweening opinion of the merits of their own country and that they are very resentful of any criticism of it.

These studies by Muralt and Voltaire served as a model for subsequent writers on England in the eighteenth century, many of whom are heavily in their debt. Above all, the warmth of their attitude towards this country and its people proved infectious. They started off that admiration for all things English which characterizes the foreign accounts of this island throughout the greater part of the century, and which in its extreme forms deserves the name of anglomania. An early example of these enthusiasts, who was actually in England at the same time as Voltaire, was the Abbé Prévost, author of the *Adventures of a Man of Quality*, the fifth volume of which embodies in the form of a novel his experiences in this country. Prévost sums up his impressions of the people thus: 'I have found them to be humane, affable, generous, capable of all the sentiments that go to make noble natures and great souls. People of worth and merit in England are such as I would wish my children, and all whom I love, to be. As to their women, where they are agreeable (and generally speaking they are so), they exceed infinitely those of all other countries in the world.'

The admiration for England which Voltaire and Muralt made fashionable was fanned by the publication of Montesquieu's *De l'esprit des lois* (1748), which did much to direct the attention of Europe to the peculiarities and advantages of the British political system. And yet, oddly enough, his *Notes sur l'Angleterre*, written during his stay in this country from 1729 to 1731, are on the whole highly critical in tone. On the one hand, England is the freest country in the world; on the other hand, 'the English are no longer worthy of their liberty. They sell it to their king, and if the king were to give it back to them, they would sell it to him again.' Corruption is universal; every vote is for sale. 'Money is rated highly here; honour and virtue little.'

Montesquieu had no great opinion of London. The streets were frightful, dirty and so ill-paved that you took your life in your hands every time you drove through them. He liked the parks, but found little to admire in the architecture. He sums up his impressions thus: 'It seems to me that Paris is a beautiful city with some ugly things; London an ugly city with some beautiful things.' The gloom of the climate oppressed him, and he had no difficulty in understanding why the English are so given to suicide.

The English are a coarse-grained people. 'The ordinary Englishman must have a good dinner, a woman and comfort. So long as he has the means of getting these he is contented; if these means fail him, he either kills himself or turns thief.' They are, too, justly famous for their cold reserve. 'It is a lamentable thing to hear the complaints of foreigners, and especially of the French, about life in London. They say that they cannot make a friend, and that the longer they stay there, the fewer friends they have, and that their civilities are received as insults. But', he asks, 'how can you expect the English to love foreigners, when they do not even love each other?'

All the visitors we have discussed so far have been either French or Swiss, and certainly in the first half of the eighteenth century it is they who set the tone. But in the later decades of the century the German travellers far outweigh, in quantity if not in quality, those of any other nation. Their intellectual curiosity, their indefatigable zeal, combine to make them thorough and on the whole accurate observers of the English scene. In Germany,

England became the rage even more than in France. English literature, the English political system, English trade and manufactures, English scenery, all were the object of their admiration. The seeds of anglomania which had been sown by Voltaire and Muralt flowered far more luxuriantly among them than among Voltaire's own countrymen. By the sixties and seventies indeed England had taken the place of France as the cultural ideal of intelligent Germans and as the country most worth visiting for the serious student of human affairs.

At first this admiration was reasonably objective, but in some of the later travellers, when it was reinforced by the sentimental tendencies of the time, it becomes almost hysterical. A good example of this is the gushing Sophie von la Roche, a novelist and blue-stocking, who visited this country in 1786 and wrote an entertaining diary of her experiences. She clearly set out for England with the determination to find everything perfect. Her first act on stepping ashore was to pick up a 'little black shell, which had a value for me, *because it was on English soil.*' And when she is about to leave the country she is moved by the sight of the sea at Dover to the hope that it will always protect the inhabitants of this 'much-blessed isle' from harmful contamination by other peoples, proceeding in a kind of litany to beg that their good qualities — their noble ambition, their no less noble artistic taste, their respect for law, etc. — be preserved to them for all time. After praying that England may for ever be vouchsafed a monarch as fatherly as George III and a queen as learned and virtuous as Charlotte of Mecklenburg, and that the spirit of Chatham may descend upon her ministers, Sophie closes her peroration somewhat unexpectedly by calling upon Providence to grant 'life eternal to the Society for the Promotion of Agriculture and the Useful Arts'.

And so it is throughout. Everything fans her ardour, from the Royal Family down to the agricultural implements. The sight of Wedgwood's pottery moves her to exclaim: 'It is not partiality but the simple truth that the Briton is born for all that is noble. For as soon as his spirit can go its own way and act independently it pursues in everything the path of greatness, simplicity and beauty.' But it is where her heart is directly touched that she rises to the wildest heights of enthusiasm. The thought of London's Foundling and other hospitals leads her to apostrophize the city thus: 'Faults thou must have, because thou art inhabited by human beings, and because imperfection is our common lot: but how much that is good, how much that is excellent resides in thee, in small things and great, for the common weal. The blessings of my affectionate heart remain with thee to the end of the world.'

What, we may ask, were the qualities of our nation which called forth such raptures? In the first place, they were the same characteristics which had evoked the approval of Muralt and Voltaire. Thus England is above all the land of common sense. 'It reigns in every branch of government, in all the great national institutions, in commerce, in literature, and in everything that constitutes the predominant character of a people', writes the Baron Bielfeld, who was attached to the Prussian Embassy in London in 1740. 'If I had children and means', says the Göttingen Professor Lichtenberg, 'I would send them to England up to their fifteenth year, until the capacity to think for themselves had become a habit and their natural common sense had been firmly established.'

The other characteristic which never fails to impress the travellers is the English love of liberty as expressed in the Constitution and in many traits and customs of the people. Closely connected with this is their sense of political responsibility and public spirit. The behaviour of the crowd at the Westminster by-election in 1782 moves the Prussian school teacher, Carl Philip Moritz, to exclaim: 'O, my friend, when you see how the lowest menial here displays an interest in public affairs, how the smallest children share in the spirit of the nation; in short, how every one, however humble, is proud to declare that he too is a man and an Englishman as good as the king and his ministers — then, I assure you, you have a very different feeling from that produced by the sight of our soldiers drilling in Berlin.'

The visitors often express amazement at the freedom with which the people refer to their sovereign. Moritz comments on the unpopularity of George III after the American War and the extraordinary interest manifested in Frederick the Great. 'How often have I heard people exclaim: Our king is a blockhead! at the same time praising the King of Prussia to the skies. He may have a small head, they say, but he's got a hundred times more sense in it than the King of England in his thick one!'

The same spirit finds expression in the free mingling of the classes. Here is what the Abbé Prévost has to say on the subject:

> St. James's Park is the public walk of London and open to all ranks, and it is a strange sight, in fine weather, to see the flower of the nobility and the first ladies of the Court mingling in confusion with the vile populace. Such is the taste of the English, who pride themselves on this as a part of what they call their liberty. Who would dream, for instance, that the most wretched porter will dispute the wall with a lord, knowing his quality, and if both are stubborn and refuse to yield, they will come publicly to blows and fight till the strongest remain master of the pavement.

Prévost is critical of this trait, but most of the foreign visitors welcome it as an example of our truly democratic spirit.

If there is one characteristic which calls forth more comment than any other in foreign accounts of England in the eighteenth century it is our national pride. This may be partly a legacy from previous ages, for from the fourteenth century onwards few travellers to this country failed to remark on this trait. Some of the visitors find it praiseworthy and contrast it favourably with the state of affairs in their own country. The Abbé Le Blanc, for instance, who came here in 1737, writes: 'A Frenchman seems to esteem his nation only with respect to himself; an Englishman appears not to set any value on himself, but with respect to his nation; which gives an air of vanity to the one, and to the other an air of greatness.' Similarly Wendeborn, who was pastor of the German church on Ludgate Hill for over twenty years, finds that the Englishman's high opinion of himself is founded, not on his own merits, but on those of his country — to which he adds the rueful comment that in his own fatherland exactly the opposite is the case. Archenholz, Prussian soldier, historian and journalist, who wrote a popular guide to England in 1785, holds that the chief difference between the national pride of the English and that of other nations lies in the simple fact that in the case of the English it is deserved.

But many foreign commentators find more to blame than to praise in this characteristic, for it is only too apt to degenerate into national arrogance and ignorant contempt for other peoples. This xenophobia is specially directed against the French, for whom the English have no good word. 'French dog' was a common term of abuse, and anyone with an outlandish look was apt to have it, or worse, flung at him, as he walked through the streets of London.

Another characteristic of the English which few travellers omit to mention is their tendency to 'Spleen', a quality which they interpret as a mixture between melancholy and eccentricity. One of the symptoms of this is the extra-ordinary penchant of the English for suicide. One visitor after another refers to this foible — for as such the English seem to regard it. Indeed at this period we evidently enjoyed the reputation of being the most suicidal of all peoples. The reasons suggested to explain this tendency vary greatly, from the gloom of the English climate to an excess of butcher's meat.

This tendency could be considered as one aspect of the astounding intrepidity or rather indifference of the English in the face of death, a subject to which the travellers also recur again and again. An extreme form of this is manifested in the public executions at Tyburn, which constituted one of the most popular spectacles of seventeenth- and eighteenth-century London. Perhaps the most vivid account of this macabre entertainment comes from Misson de Valbourg, a French Huguenot refugee, whose book on England was published in 1698:

The English are people that laugh at the delicacy of other nations, who make it such a mighty matter to be hanged; their extraordinary courage looks upon it as a trifle, and they also make a jest of the pretended dishonour that, in the opinion of others, falls upon their kindred. He that is to be hanged, or otherwise executed, first takes care to get himself shaved, and handsomely dressed, either in mourning or in the dress of a bridegroom. This done, he sets his friends at work to get him leave to be buried, and to carry his coffin with him, which is easily obtained. When his suit of clothes, or night-gown, his gloves, hat, periwig, nosegay, coffin, flannel-dress for his corpse, and all such are bought and prepared, the main point is taken care of, his mind is at peace, and then he thinks of his conscience.

Misson's account may sound exaggerated, but it is borne out by many other travellers. Eccentricity, indeed, as Muralt had remarked, is a notable ingredient of the English make-up. Foreign visitors give many instances of this. One of the most delectable is recorded by a young Alsatian merchant, Eberhard Zetzner. When in London in 1700 he saw three men running naked through the streets, who had vowed to wear no clothes nor cut their hair until King James II should be restored to his throne. He adds that they are said to be of good family, and 'their skin is black as earth'.

Despite the prevalent anglomania, the picture of our country presented by the foreign visitor, even before the French Revolution, is by no means entirely favourable. After our national arrogance and insularity, it is our coarse brutality which evokes the most frequent criticism. Examples of this are the crude sports which play so large a part in English life: the bull- and bear-baitings, the cock fights, the boxing and wrestling matches. César de Saussure, a Swiss of French Huguenot origin who was in England from 1725 to 1729, has left a horrific account of a gladiatorial combat between two women. These Amazons fought almost naked with two-handed swords which were sharp as razors at the ends. The spectators, who included several peers, laid wagers on the result of the fight. Blood soon began to flow freely. One of the combatants received a great gash across the forehead which had to be sewn up before she could return to the fray. Finally 'she received a long and deep wound all across her neck and throat. The surgeon sewed her up again, but she was too badly hurt to fight any more, and it was high time too, for the combatants were dripping with blood and perspiration.' These gladiatorial combats, usually, it is true, between men, appear to have been common in the early decades of the century, and several travellers have left vivid accounts of them.

In keeping with the crudity of our sports is the crudity of our manners. This was an aspect of the national character which, as we might expect, specially struck the visitors from France. François de la Rochefoucauld, who visited this country in 1784, describes the post-prandial habits of the English gentleman:

Conversation is as free as it can be, everyone expresses his political opinions with as much frankness as he would employ upon personal subjects. Sometimes conversation becomes extremely free upon highly indecent topics — complete licence is allowed, and I have come to the conclusion that the English do not associate the same ideas with certain words that we do. Very often I have heard things mentioned in good society which would be in the grossest taste in France. The side-board too is furnished with a number of chamber-pots and it is a common practice to relieve oneself while the rest are drinking; one has no kind of concealment and the practice strikes me as most indecent.

The amusements of the town naturally play a large part in the visitors' observations. The Baron Pöllnitz, far-travelled and frivolous, thinks highly of London as a city of pleasure, and does not agree with those Frenchified and Italianized Englishmen who prefer the claims of Paris or Rome. He describes the typical day of a man about town in the reign of George I. He rises late, strolls to the Park, returns home to change, and then saunters to the coffee-house — for it is a sort of law with the English to visit one of these haunts at least once a day, and there talk business or politics, read the papers or — more often — gaze at each other in silence. At one o'clock he goes to Court and at three he dines. After dinner, if the weather is fine, he takes the air, by coach in Hyde Park or on foot in St

James's, and in winter pays calls till the play begins. After
the play he attends the Assembly or the Drawing-room,
and at midnight takes supper, at which 'Bacchus est
ordinairement secondé par Vénus' — and so to bed.
Believe me, he adds, it is pure affectation to pretend that
life in London is boring.

We hear a good deal of the London stage from the
travellers. Many of them saw Garrick at the height of his
powers and fame and have left some vivid descriptions of
his acting. At the end of the century Mrs Siddons called
forth almost equal enthusiasm. But going to the theatre
was not without its inconveniences. The rowdiness of the
audience never ceased to astonish foreign visitors. The
Abbé Le Blanc remarks in 1737:

> Half an hour before the play was to begin the spectators
> gave notice of their dispositions by frightful hisses and out-
> cries, equal perhaps to what were ever heard in a Roman
> amphitheatre. I could not have known but by my eyes only
> that I was among an assembly of beings who thought them-
> selves to be reasonable. The author, who had foreseen the
> fury of the pit, took care to be armed against it. He knew
> what people he had to deal with; and, to make them easy,
> put in his prologue double the usual dose of incense that is
> offered to their vanity.

Things do not seem to have improved much in this respect
by the end of the century. A German traveller records in
1791 that at Drury Lane a rowdiness and disorder prevail
such as would have disgraced a puppet-show in a village
barn in his fatherland.

On the whole it is surprising how little the political
events of the century are reflected in the travel journals.
Occasionally we get a vivid touch, as when the Baron
Bielfeld observes Sir Robert Walpole nibbling apples in
the House of Commons while waiting to speak, which he

is usually one of the last to do. Another traveller in 1788 notices the inscription chalked on windows which had been blocked up owing to the window tax: 'Lighten our darkness, O Pitt!'

The loss of the American colonies, it is true, leaves its trace on several of the later travel journals. There are Cassandra-like prophecies of England's impending decline after having reached the zenith of her power and prosperity. The size of the national debt must lead inevitably to national bankruptcy; at the same time moral corruption and luxurious living are paving the way for her eclipse.

But it was the French Revolution which first brought about a fundamental change in the attitude of the foreign visitors to this island. Hitherto England had been accepted as the land of freedom *par excellence*. And now suddenly the tables were turned. Not only was this monopoly in liberty challenged by the French Revolution, but the freer France became, the more repressive, it seemed, grew England. For the fear of revolutionary principles spreading to their own country had forced the English Government under Pitt to adopt measures — such as the suspension of the Habeas Corpus Act and the censorship of the press — which considerably curtailed the freedom of which Englishmen had been so proud. From being the land of liberty England had become in the eyes of many the home of tyranny and oppression.

This change in the attitude of the travellers is perhaps most clearly illustrated in the writings of Archenholz, who has already been referred to as an anglophil. In 1787 he writes: 'It is an acknowledged truth that no civilized nation was ever so free as the people of England are at this day.' But already in 1790 he complains that he, the former eulogist of British freedom, is forced as a historian to

record that 'their ever more and more restricted liberty
can no longer stand comparison with the French.' And
nine years later he exclaims in disgust: 'England is now
like a prison, at whose portals brutal and fearful inquisi-
tors are stationed.'

And so under the pressure of events the anglomania of
the seventies and eighties gradually gave way to a more
critical and even hostile attitude, which in extreme cases
amounted to an anglophobia just as hysterical as the anglomania it supplanted. The best example we possess of a
good hater of this country is the Prussian preacher and
journalist, Andreas Riem, whose *Travels* (1796–1801)
afford an extreme instance of this reaction. Riem expresses
the situation in uncompromising terms. 'While the des-
pised Frenchman threw off the yoke of servitude and did
not hesitate to give his life for freedom, a people far-
famed for its love of liberty allowed itself to be chained in
slavish despotism by a minister and his representatives.'
There is only one thing about this country that meets with
Riem's approval, and that is the landscape. All the more
painful, then, is the contrast with its inhabitants, 'a debased species of humanity, which one must know personally
in order to despise as they deserve. Pride and ignorance,
brutality and opulent display, insolence and treachery,
vice in its wildest excesses amounting to infamy — these
are the unvarnished characteristics of a people that in-
habits the Garden of Eden.'

Hundreds of pages are devoted to proving that the un-
sound system of over-taxation and the extent of England's
liabilities in all parts of the world, occasioned by her greed
and by the loss of the American colonies, have brought the
nation to the verge of bankruptcy. Anyone willing to lend
money to such a country is fit only for the madhouse. In
striking contrast to this situation and to the general weak-

ness of her policy are the monstrous pretensions of England as a belligerent power, especially her claim to the command of the seas, which he calls 'the most arrogant piece of insolence under the sun'. As one would expect, Riem is much preoccupied with the supposed merits of the British Constitution. In his view this is in fact a concealed despotism of the most evil kind, in which the people, under the pretence of freedom, are the victims of a tyranny which is not only unscrupulous but corrupt and incompetent to the last degree.

After this it is no surprise to learn that the national character itself is the quintessence of all that is bad. Riem pours scorn on the attributes which are usually applied to it. 'If you want magnanimity, justice and humanity, then do not look for them in England.' The basic evil of the English character is materialism, the commercial spirit, which is the enemy of all the virtues and which throttles all feelings that cannot be measured in terms of hard cash. To such a people sympathy and humanity must appear as weakness, altruism as raving folly, and virtue a thing of nought. This and the melancholic temperament induced by the climate he makes responsible for most of the characteristics of the English who, in his opinion, 'lag far behind most European nations in moral and other respects; in reality, they are little better than coarse, crude, uncouth, arrogant, half-savage barbarians.'

But Riem is an exception. The overwhelming majority of foreign visitors to England in the eighteenth century find much more to praise than to blame. At no period of our history apparently was the rest of the civilized world, despite national rivalries, so warmly disposed towards us. Was the reason perhaps the simple one that never before or since have we had so much in civilized values to offer the rest of the world?

SUGGESTIONS FOR READING

Letts, M., *As the Foreigner saw us*, Methuen, 1935.

Robson-Scott, W. D., *German Travellers in England, 1400–1800*, Blackwell, 1953.

Wilson, F. M., *Strange Island. Britain through Foreign Eyes, 1395–1940*, Longmans, 1955.

Saussure, C. de, *A Foreign View of England in the Reigns of George I and George II*, translated by Madame van Muyden, Murray, 1902.

Moritz, C. P., *Travels in England in 1782*, edited by P. E. Matheson, Humphrey Milford, 1924.

Voltaire, F. M. A. de., *Letters concerning the English Nation*, edited by Charles Whibley, Davies, 1926.

Prévost, A. F., *Adventures of a Man of Quality*, translated and edited by M. E. I. Robertson, Routledge, 1930.

La Roche, Sophie von, *Sophie in London, 1786*, translated and edited by C. Williams, Cape, 1933.

Muralt, B. L. de, *Lettres sur les Anglois et les François*, edited by C. Gould, Paris, 1933.

Rochefoucauld, F. de la, *A Frenchman in England, 1784*, translated and edited by S. C. Roberts, Cambridge University Press, 1933.

Lichtenberg, G. C., *Lichtenberg's Visits to England*, translated and edited by M. L. Mare and W. H. Quarrel, Clarendon Press, 1938.

XI

Science in Eighteenth-Century Britain

by COLIN A. RONAN

EIGHTEENTH-century British science, like that of the century before, was dominated by the name of Isaac Newton, a man whose work has often been said to be unique and to have surpassed that of all other scientific men. Certainly his greatest contribution to our knowledge of the world and what lies beyond it was published in his famous *Philosophiæ Naturalis Principia Mathematica* (Mathematical Principles of Natural Philosophy, usually called 'the *Principia*' for short), and it opened up a new approach to man's understanding of the world and of the universe. Because of this we must begin by seeing exactly what it is that he achieved. From the dawn of the earliest civilizations in Egypt and Mesopotamia (or Iraq, as it is now called) man had felt that the stars and planets were something not only beyond his reach, but also beyond his complete understanding. Clearly they were different from things on Earth — from generation to generation they never underwent any apparent change — and the general ideas which were developed about the behaviour of material bodies were thought to be something which applied only to the Earth itself. The laws which governed the heavens were, it was believed, essentially different. Newton's great 'break through' was that he saw that the same laws which operate on the Earth operate also in the farthest depths of space. Moreover, he formulated this by his theory of 'universal gravitation', using precise mathematical arguments.

To bring, as Newton did, the motion of the Moon under the same laws of behaviour as a falling apple, or a horse and cart, was an immense step forward and affected man's whole scientific outlook. Of course others before Newton had been working along this path, but the lanes they had travelled were ill-lit and shadowy. What they had discovered, however, was that one could take earthly things and, by carefully arranging what happened to them, weigh and measure the results, and then approach new knowledge by means of experiment. This experimental attitude is, of course, the touchstone of science as we now understand it, and really separates what is called 'modern science' from that which, for thousands of years, had preceded it. Newton acknowledged the work of others. As he himself said, he 'stood on the shoulders of giants', and in doing so broke through the barrier which had hitherto existed between things on Earth and things elsewhere. So great an advance had all kinds of effects not only on astronomy and physics but also on man's understanding of, for example, the working of the human body.

Newton's contribution to 'natural knowledge' — as science was then called — did not rest with the *Principia*, although he continually revised it so that, while the first edition was published in 1687, a second edition, with certain changes, came out in 1713, and a third edition in 1726, one year before his death. He worked also on optics and the nature of light, and was the first to show that daylight or 'white light' is actually composed of all colours. The main part of his book *Opticks* was concerned with the question of coloured light, although it dealt also with the laws of reflection and refraction, and contained his ideas on the nature of light itself. Newton worked for many years on these problems, conducted many experiments, and published some of his ideas in the scientific journal of the Royal Society known as the *Philosophical Transactions*. The *Opticks* was first published in 1704 and, like the *Principia*, came out in later editions, containing new ideas, in 1717, 1721 and, in an edition 'corrected by the author's own hand', in 1730.

A contemporary and friend of Newton's who must be mentioned was the astronomer Edmond Halley. Halley is now remembered for his discovery of a great comet which bears his name. He was the first to apply Newton's ideas of universal gravitation as put forward in *Principia*, thus being able to calculate with considerable accuracy the path of the comet, and envisage that it moved round the Sun in a closed path, so that he was able to 'predict' its return. Yet it was not for his cometary work that Halley was famous in his own day. He was, of course, widely known for his astronomical work, and in 1720 he became the second Astronomer Royal, succeeding John Flamsteed, who had held the post since its creation by Charles II in 1675. Halley was a man of unbounded energy. It was he who first began a study of the Earth as a physical body, and he can well be called the first geophysicist. He took command of a ship of the Royal Navy and charted the magnetic variation over the Atlantic Ocean, using a means for showing this on maps which is still the basis of the method used today. Halley was also a man of great tact, and it was due to him that Newton was first stimulated to write the *Principia* and to keep on with the task when, because of arguments with others, he wanted to shelve the whole work. It was Halley who actually paid for its publication out of his own pocket, and carried out the laborious task of seeing the work properly printed. Halley did many other things besides his astronomical and mathematical work, including running a public company for salvaging wrecks, and he invented a diving helmet and himself went down in it, not forgetting of course to write to Newton and tell him of the colours of sunlight as seen at various depths. Halley, like Newton, also worked at the Royal Mint during the re-coinage which was carried out in the reign of William and Mary.

Above all Halley was a great astronomer, and contributed much to the immense developments in science which were taking place in the eighteenth century. The discovery of the telescope some thirty years before the beginning of the century had brought a notable advance in the precision with which measures of the position of stars and planets could be made. Halley mapped many of the stars visible only in the southern sky, and also discovered that the stars, always believed truly fixed in space, actually had individual motions of their own. He also developed a new and more accurate way for determining the distance of the Sun. The eighteenth century also saw the work of Flamsteed, the first Astronomer Royal, who ably began the accuracy of measurement for which the Royal Greenwich Observatory has always been famous, and the labours of John Bradley, who became the third Astronomer Royal in 1742, when he succeeded Halley. Bradley discovered an apparent motion of the stars which was, he found, due both to the speed with which light travels and the motion of the Earth in its orbit round the Sun and, incidentally, was thus the first to prove experimentally that the Earth moved in space. Among others who helped in the development of astronomy were Chester Moor Hall who, with the assistance of the optician John Dolland, produced the achromatic telescope — that is, a telescope which did not give the coloured fringes to objects seen through it which so marred the efficiency of earlier instruments — and Thomas Wright of Durham, who suggested that the stars were distributed through space in certain directions only, and that beyond them lay what seemed to be clouds of gas which astronomers named 'nebulae'. Wright was much advanced in his views, and it was not until the nineteenth century that his ideas bore fruit.

Probably the greatest of the eighteenth-century astronomers, and certainly the greatest observational astronomer of all time, was William Herschel. Born in Hanover and trained as a professional musician, Herschel came to England in 1757 and followed a musical career. However, his heart became wedded to astronomy. His observing began in Bath, using reflecting telescopes made, literally, by his own hands. He was a wonderful telescope maker, his instruments being widely acknowledged as by far the best then available, and in his lifetime he constructed the incredible total of 430 telescope mirrors. Herschel was the first to use a telescope for a systematic study of the sky. In 1781 he was rewarded by the discovery of the planet Uranus. This was a notable advance, for the five planets — Mercury, Venus, Mars, Jupiter and Saturn — had been known from earliest times, and in discovering Uranus Herschel was the first man since written history to find a new planet. It was Herschel, too, who discovered the existence of variable stars and of double stars which revolved round each other and were a demonstration of the Newtonian principle of universal gravitation operating right out in the depths of space; he discovered also the motion of the Sun in space. His surveys of the entire northern heavens were a monument to his indefatigable labours, which in 1786 were recognized by George III, who provided him with a royal pension and the position of 'Court Astronomer'.

These great steps in astronomical discovery, following

directly on the developments of Newton's ideas and the discovery of the telescope, allied to the experimental approach to new knowledge, had a profound effect on man's work in other scientific fields, an effect which gradually gained momentum during the eighteenth century. Halley's work on the magnetic field of the Earth in the last ten years of the previous century was followed up in 1724 by Graham who, after careful observations, discovered the daily or diurnal variation of the compass. Experiments were also carried out in the allied study of electricity. Hawksbee observed the glow which occurred in the partly-evacuated glass tube of a mercury barometer, originally discovered by the Frenchman Picard. Picard had suggested that this was due to the existence of phosphorus, but Hawksbee in 1705 realized that it was due to the existence of an electric 'virtue' caused by the friction between the mercury and the glass of the tube. This discovery showed the possibility of the existence of electricity in metals, and stimulated interest for further studies. Matters were taken a step forward by Stephen Gray. Gray was a great experimenter, and his work was concerned with rubbing various substances and noting not only the presence of electric 'virtue' but also the distance from the electrified object to which the 'virtue' could still be observed. He was really the inventor of the electroscope which we can still see in use in physics laboratories today, and he discovered that the 'virtue' could be transmitted great distances along silk thread and also that it could be induced in one body from another. His work had great influence on later developments, but the idea of electric 'virtue' gave place to the suggestion of electricity being a fluid which could be neither weighed nor measured. Work on the electroscope continued throughout the century, and contributions were made by Henry Cavendish and by Bennet, who invented the gold-leaf electroscope in the form we now know it. However, the other really great work in electrical studies which took place during the century was by Cavendish and Joseph Priestley, who studied with great care to find the law governing the force between electric charges. It was, of course, important that such a relationship should be discovered if electricity was to become a precise study, and the experiments of Cavendish and Priestley helped the Frenchman Coulomb, who actually managed to enunciate the law.

Another mystery of the time was the question of heat. What was it? Could it be a fluid which although having neither mass nor any other detectable quality was, nevertheless, transferred from a cold body to a hot one? Clearly, before making up a theory it was necessary to find out as many facts as possible. Newton and Halley, at the beginning of the century, were both aware that water boiled at an almost constant temperature, while their colleague Robert Hooke knew that ice always melted at a constant temperature, and in the century before had distinguished between fire and flames, which he realized were due to the action of heated bodies with air, and heat itself which, he suggested, arose from the motion of the various parts of which he believed bodies to be composed. Newton, at the end of his *Opticks*, in which he posed many queries on various physical problems, also suggested that heat was due to the movement of the particles of a body and, further, that when a body was much heated the vibration of these very particles caused light to be emitted. Newton gave as examples the repeated hammering of iron, which could cause it to glow with a dull red heat. It was, however, on the Continent that the idea of heat as an 'imponderable fluid' found favour, and this view was the one most widely held during the eighteenth century.

One of the great British scientists of this period to work on these problems was Joseph Black. He was the first to appreciate the difference between the *quantity* of heat in a body and the *intensity* of heat which a body 'contained'. As an example Black pointed out that, if a block of iron and a block of wood were both removed from the same oven, the iron would feel hotter for a longer time than the wood, and argued that this showed that, although the intensity of heat in both bodies would be the same, the quantity stored in the iron would be more than that stored in the wood. Black also put forward the theory that the capacity of a body for storing heat depended on the change of heat intensity which such a body would undergo when placed in contact with a body of different capacity. He also exploded the idea, widely held in the middle of the century, that only a little heat was needed to raise a body from freezing to the point when it thawed. Quoting as examples the effort needed to melt ice, and the existence even during summer of ice on the tops of mountains, he concluded that much heat was required to cause a change of state of material from freezing to thawing. We now know that he was absolutely correct. Black also investigated the change from liquid to vapour which happens when a substance boils. He found also that much heat must be put into a body to cause this change, and concluded that the quantities of heat to cause a change of state built up in a body until the change occurred; for this he coined the name 'Latent Heat' — a name still used today.

The other important work on heat in eighteenth-century Britain was on the relation between mechanical effort and heat generated because of it. The British contribution came late in the century and acted as a basis for much that followed in other countries; it was due to the work of Benjamin Thompson (Count Rumford). Thompson had a chequered career, for he organized much of the Bavarian army, was a Count of the Holy Roman Empire, and in England he founded the Royal Institution. It was while working for the Bavarian army at Munich that he watched the boring of cannon and recorded his observations in a scientific paper entitled 'Source of Heat Excited by Friction'. After this he carried out a number of experiments. In one he bored a metal cylinder, carefully measured the heat generated, and worked out the quantity of ice which such heat would melt. In another experiment he surrounded a cylinder with water and noted how long boring had to continue before the water boiled. From these investigations Thompson realized that the quantity of heat which could be generated appeared to be inexhaustible and depended only on the mechanical work done. In consequence he concluded that heat could not be thought of as a material substance, or even an imponderable fluid, and suggested that it must be caused by a motion of particles. Thus the fluid theory of heat received a death blow, and Thompson's discoveries paved the way for others on the Continent who, in the nineteenth century, continued along these lines.

There is, of course, another aspect of heat — that which is concerned when bodies are burnt. Flames are often seen, and during combustion bodies appear to lose something. To account for this the 'phlogiston' theory was put forward, primarily by the German Stahl. It was an attempt to explain the observed facts, and 'phlogiston' was thought of as a substance which is driven off when bodies are burnt. We know now that the confusion which led to the acceptance of this theory was due to the fact that no one at the time realized that gases were given off or taken up by a body during combustion — indeed the idea of a gas had not been thought of. It was of course known that air was affected, but air was believed to be of one substance only. The overthrow of the 'phlogiston' theory finally took place in France in the latter part of the century, and among those who contributed to this by their experiments and discoveries were a number of British chemists. The first of these was Stephen Hales, who heated a great variety of substances, collected the 'air' which was given off, and weighed it. He concluded that 'air' was contained in all materials, but he never examined the chemical nature of the 'air', only its physical properties. By the middle of the century an important step was taken by Joseph Black, who concluded from various experiments that there *was* another 'aerial' substance besides 'air'. Following on the work of Hales and Black, Henry Cavendish studied what had come to be thought of as two kinds of air. Again his approach was concerned with the physical properties of these airs. However, by 1766 three kinds of air were recognized, but the differences between them were thought of as physical, not chemical.

Another very accurate and careful observer, Joseph Priestley, worked on the problem. He held to the idea that there were many airs of different kinds, and that 'phlogiston' was the most satisfactory explanation, although, to his credit, he also appreciated that there might be some other satisfactory theory, and the experimental evidence which he accumulated was of use to others on the Continent who studied the problem. This work was followed by more experiments which, among other things, led, in due course, to the then novel idea of naming materials because of the chemicals contained in them; thus a name like butter of antimony became antimony chloride, and really described the substance. The new names were published in 1789 in a book by the Frenchman Lavoisier, of which an edition in English appeared in 1790, but before this date Joseph

Black in Edinburgh was already teaching them to his students! All these careful observations and experiments made in Britain began to bear fruit, and helped to usher in a new precision in the study of chemistry.

The whole question of naming or classifying things is very important in science, and reflects the understanding which underlies a subject. This is especially so in the studies of the diversity of the animals and plants with which the world is populated, and it was in the eighteenth century that a new approach was made to this problem. By this time it was appreciated that animals and plants can be classified either by the way they are made or reproduce their young, or by the way they live in their surroundings. Each point of view expresses an important fact, and our choice may well colour the way in which we deal with things. One system of classifying animals was put forward by John Ray. He decided to divide animals into two groups, those with blood (e.g. mammals, birds, reptiles, fish) and those without (e.g. molluscs, crustaceans and insects). This was a bold attempt; and he also published a classification of plants using the fruit, flower, leaf and other characteristics, and gave a system of orders of plants many of which are still in use. His work was taken up by the Swede Carl von Linné (usually known as Linnaeus) who introduced the terms *genus* and *species*. Ray also noted that some creatures did not seem to be perfectly adapted to their surroundings, and he attempted to explain this by a 'plastic nature' which he supposed caused alterations from the basic 'design' with which animals had originally been provided. Ray's work had an effect on the theory of evolution which became very much developed in the next century. So also did the ideas of Erasmus Darwin. Darwin was a great believer in progress, and he put forward the idea that structure was the basis of animal form but that the functions and capabilities of animals were dependent upon their surroundings. Darwin's proposal was, in essence, one of emergent evolution, yet his ideas were but a glimpse of the theory which was to be put forward so fully by his grandson, Charles Darwin, in the nineteenth century.

These studies of types of creatures and their development went hand in hand with work on the anatomy of man and animals. Edward Tyson, whose work began in the seventeenth century, carried out a systematic dissection of animals in order to compare one with another, while Martin Lister carefully studied the construction of slugs, snails and molluscs, and another Englishman, Nehemiah Grew, examined the alimentary canal, that passage through the body which is concerned with the intake and digestion of food and disposal of waste products. But the most outstanding anatomist of the century was John Hunter, who qualified at St George's Hospital, London, and whose bust can still be seen outside the students' entrance in Knightsbridge. Hunter was a brilliant surgeon — for example, he devised a new operation for local swelling of the arteries which superseded the usual operation made in his day which had been evolved 1500 years before — he was, in fact, the inventor of scientific surgery and also of modern dentistry. His studies were wide in scope; he was interested in the natural temperatures of animals, the electric organs of certain fishes, the structure of whales, the use of the air sacs in birds, and even the behaviour of bees and the hibernation of animals. He collected many anatomical specimens as well as animals and plants of all kinds, arranging these to illustrate the comparative anatomy and physiology of the animal and plant kingdoms. Hunter also studied the blood, and in 1794 wrote a book about it which contained many

H

revolutionary ideas, and he was much interested in those diseases caused by loose living. He invented a method for injection, and injected himself with one of these diseases in order the better to study it. Unfortunately he contracted two diseases, and it cost him his life. He left his many unpublished writings to a distant relation, who passed off some of them as his own work and burnt the remainder, so it is not easy to be certain of all that John Hunter achieved. It is, however, clear that his work had a great effect on future developments, developments which were to lead to advances in surgery, in inoculation, and in the appreciation of the reasons for many diseases. The idea that germs can cause disease, and that often such diseases are air-borne, was not then appreciated, although in 1720 some surprising work was carried out by Benjamin Marten. He suggested that consumption was due to the entry into the lungs *via* the air of tiny living creatures which he believed would wound and gnaw 'tender vessels in the lungs' and so cause ulceration. Marten gave what, in fact, was an excellent description of tuberculosis and its cause but, unfortunately, his ideas were at least a century ahead of their time, and no one followed them up.

We can see then that in the eighteenth century the breadth and scope of British science was something in which we can take pride. In London the Royal Society, the oldest and most active scientific society in the world, flourished. Everyone mentioned in this chapter was a Fellow of it, and most contributed to the *Philosophical Transactions* in which, even to this day, new scientific knowledge is announced. We had, during the Silver Renaissance, a record of scientific achievement which was second to none, and which continued to go forward and so increase Man's understanding of the universe in which he finds himself, and contribute to the well-being of mankind.

SUGGESTIONS FOR FURTHER READING

Pledge, H. T., *Science since 1500*, H.M.S.O., 1939. Not recommended for reading, but useful for dates and diagrams.

Singer, C., *A Short History of Science*, Clarendon Press, 1941.

Dampier, W. C., *Shorter History of Science*, Cambridge University Press, 1944.

Butterfield, H., *The Origin of Modern Science*, Bell, 1949.

Crombie, A. C., *Augustine to Galileo*, Falcon Educational Books, 1952.

Dingle, H., *The Scientific Adventure*, Pitman, 1952. In the first part of this book there are some very worthwhile essays. The second part will probably be found too difficult.

Mason, S. F., *A History of the Sciences*, Routledge & Kegan Paul, 1953.

XII

The Electorate of Hanover

by ALEX NATAN

AT 7.15 on the morning of August 1, 1714, Anne, Queen of England, died, and the personal union of England with the German Electorate of Hanover came into being. The successor to Anne on the British throne was the Elector of Brunswick-Lüneburg, George Louis, who on August 31 left his capital for England. Hanover, the residential city of the Electors, gave its name to the new dynasty, and until the accession of Queen Victoria the kings of England bore a patronymic derived from the city George Louis had left to become George I of England.

Originally Hanover had been no more than the capital of the Dukedom of Calenberg. It is described in Merian's *Topography*, which dates from about 1654:

> The town of Hanover is well guarded by high, strong walls, ramparts, bastions, and a deep moat. For further protection, the inner wall has thirty-six towers spaced along it. Within the walls are four long and very wide streets which, like the side streets, are well cobbled. From time immemorial it has also had a deservedly famous school. For over a hundred years, the livelihood of the citizens has come from divers trades, businesses and crafts, but first and foremost from the brewing of a good wholesome beer, called locally 'Brühan', which still flourishes. Furthermore, for remaining loyal and true to each successive Prince in the troubled times of the past, the town and citizenry have been rewarded with con-

siderable privileges — for example, the 'mero et mixto imperio' and other exceptional benefits. And these privileges have been confirmed and ratified up to the present time.

In 1692, after a long and bitter struggle, Ernest Augustus became Elector of Brunswick-Lüneburg, a position which entitled him to vote in the Imperial Elections of the Holy Roman Empire. Hanover then became the capital of the new Electorate, the ninth in the German Empire. When Ernest Augustus married Sophia, granddaughter of James I, there arose the very distant possibility that the House of Hanover might one day lay claim to the English throne. George Louis, son of Ernest Augustus and Sophia, succeeded his father when the latter died in 1698, and on the death of his uncle, George William of Lüneburg-Celle, he became also Duke of Lüneburg by virtue of his marriage with his cousin Sophia Dorothea, daughter of George William. Thus there came to fruition the event Ernest Augustus had long worked for — the uniting of the Dukedoms of Lüneburg and Calenberg, which formed the basis of the Electorate of Hanover.

Meanwhile the prospects of a Hanoverian succession to the English throne had improved considerably. Seldom has Fate shown herself more capricious than when, in the seventeenth century, she removed from the scene every heir who stood between George Louis's mother, the Electress Sophia, and the English throne. As Catholics, the descendants of James II had been excluded from the succession since the Declaration of Rights and the Act of Settlement. The Protestant members of the House of Stuart, Queen Mary II and Queen Anne, either had no heirs or outlived them. But Sophia, daughter of the tragic 'Queen of Hearts', Elizabeth of Bohemia, was not destined to profit by Fate's generosity, for she died two months before Queen Anne.

The personal union of England and Hanover which began with George Louis was destined to last for 123 years, a period during which England built up her Empire. It is often thought of as a period during which the Hanoverian Kings subordinated the interests of England to those of the Electorate. German commentators, however, tend to underline the fact that the Electorate had now become an appendage, a province, of the British Empire. It is not the intention here to enlarge upon this dispute, but rather to attempt a picture of the Electorate, to define its position among the other German Electorates, its atmosphere and its cultural activities, and finally to trace the course of those tragic events which were woven into the destinies of three beautiful, gifted women of the time. Who in England at the present time is familiar with that baroque stage on which George Louis played his part, that world theatre in miniature which influenced him and on which he left his mark before becoming George I of Great Britain and Ireland? It must always be borne in mind that in Hanover George Louis had presided over a German Court that was important both politically and culturally, but which, compared with the Court of St James, was still remarkably provincial; and it sent to England a man unfamiliar with the system and set-up that prevailed there.

How and when did the Electorate of Hanover come into being? After the death of Sophia's father-in-law, Duke John Frederick, in 1679, his son Ernest Augustus succeeded to the title. He was an ambitious and highly gifted man, and it was his dearest wish to see his Dukedom of Calenberg raised to the status of an Electorate. With this in mind he prepared the way for an alliance with Lüneburg-Celle, whose Duke was his second eldest brother George William. The latter, susceptible to his brother's influence in this direction, contracted a morganatic marriage with the Frenchwoman, Eléonor d'Olbreuse. The only child of this union, Sophia Dorothea, married Ernest Augustus's son and heir, George Louis. The amalgamation of the two territories was now assured; it was only a question of time, for it would become an accomplished fact on the death of George William.

The attainment of the Electorship was not so easy. It was necessary to gain the consent of the Emperor, of the College of Electors, and of those German Princes not of electoral rank. The last provided the greatest difficulty, for they would naturally oppose the elevation of a House from among their own members. The Electors, on their side, were opposed to any increase in their numbers, and the Catholics among them endeavoured to thwart the installation of a Protestant Elector. Above these interested parties stood the Emperor, whose approval had first to be won. For a long time Leopold I obstructed the Hanoverian plans. Ernest Augustus took advantage of the delay to reform his Government and administration, thus strengthening his power. In 1682 he established the law of primogeniture in his domain. He also asked Leibniz to make formal application on his behalf for the Electoral Hat. In addition, he set aside large sums of money from his revenues with which to bribe the German Princes and buy their goodwill. At last, on March 22, 1692, he achieved his goal, and the electoral negotiations were completed and signed. The prospect of Hanoverian military aid may have helped Leopold to make his decision more easily, for he was at that time under severe pressure, with a war on two fronts, one against Louis XIV and one against the Turks. The solemn investiture of the new Elector took place in Vienna in December. Nevertheless, opposition to the Guelphs in some quarters was as strong as ever, and it was not until 1708, ten years after the death of Ernest Augustus, that his son George Louis was accepted into the College of Electors by virtue of a decree of the Imperial Diet. Here was yet another triumph for the tenacity and far-sightedness of Ernest Augustus: Hanover was now the capital of an Electorate.

Among those who had materially helped to establish the new Electorate was one of the most learned men of his time, Gottfried Wilhelm Leibniz (1646–1716). What was the relationship between the Court and the philosopher, propounder of the doctrine of monads and perfector of the differential and integral calculi? What brought him to Hanover and why did he come? The first link in the chain goes back to 1671, when Leibniz was living at the Court of the Elector of Mainz. He attracted the attention of the Hanoverian Duke John Frederick, and a correspondence began between them. On April 15, 1671, Leibniz was offered a position in Hanover. He refused it, in the hope of becoming Historiographer in Vienna. Two years later, seeing that his hopes were not going to be fulfilled, he re-opened correspondence with Hanover. In September 1676, after lengthy negotiations, John Frederick offered Leibniz the position of Director of the Library, which the Duke himself had founded, together with a salary of 600 thalers and the rank of Electoral Counsellor. Moreover Leibniz was assured of plenty of free time to pursue his own studies. He finally moved to Hanover in December. He had not only failed to achieve the position he coveted in Vienna, but the seat he had been expecting in the Académie Française had also eluded him. Financial security must have been the chief attraction of the offer that finally brought Leibniz to Hanover, but it was with a heavy heart that he entered the city. He served for a time as Electoral Counsellor, but was released from that duty and given the task of improving water-regulation in the

Harz mines. The schemes he worked out for this project unfortunately failed, which weakened his standing at Court. To improve his position, he asked the new Duke, Ernest Augustus, in 1685, to commission him to write the history of the House of Guelph. The Duke agreed, on condition that Leibniz accepted no foreign appointments, and that he commuted his salary to a life pension. This meant financial security at last, but it meant also that he was irrevocably committed to Hanover. Under the Elector George Louis Leibniz's position deteriorated still further. Freedom of travel was denied him, and an attempt was made to prevent him from setting aside time for his own studies, a privilege which had been part of his initial agreement. George Louis could never understand the difference between the work of a scholar and the duties of an official, and it was this that eventually drove Leibniz from Hanover. He had long wanted to go to Vienna, but his great work on the history of the Guelph dynasty hung round his neck like a millstone, and it was not his way to leave work unfinished. Nevertheless, at the end of 1712 he went to Vienna, without permission from his employer, and stayed there almost two years, while increasingly urgent demands for his return came from Hanover. He finally left Vienna loaded with honours, an Imperial Counsellor, and with the promise of the directorship of the proposed Academy of Science. He was given a special stipend, and promised to return on the completion of his book.

After the death of his friend the Electress Sophia, and the accession of George Louis to the English throne, Leibniz, who was suffering from gout, found Hanover a desolate place. He worked there for another two years, under thinly-veiled supervision, and died on November 16, 1716. John Ker, who was on a visit to Hanover at the time, wrote in his memoirs: 'I must confess it afforded me matter of strange reflection, when I perceived the little regard that was paid to his ashes by the Hanoverians; for he was buried in a few days after his decease, more like a robber than what he was, the ornament of his country.' The man who as mathematician, philosopher, diplomat and historian, had enjoyed the highest esteem, was politically of no consequence, and counted for nothing among George I's not very intellectual friends. The relationship between Leibniz and George I never had the personal touch that was characteristic of his friendship with Sophia and later with George II's wife, the Electoral Princess Caroline of Ansbach. This unsatisfactory state of affairs led eventually to an unedifying quarrel over the completion of the history of the House of Guelph, on which Leibniz had been working for years without giving satisfaction to the Electors. It was not a project which could bring its author any personal aggrandizement. Furthermore, Leibniz was excluded from any real political activity, as his posts as Electoral Counsellor and Historiographer had no diplomatic importance. However bright the future might seem for him if once his friend the Electress Sophia ascended the English throne, it was unlikely to materialize, in view of her great age. How acutely Leibniz was aware of this, and how little he expected from George I's elevation to the English throne, comes out clearly in the pathetic letter he wrote to the Electoral Princess on Sophia's death, in which he asks her either to accept him as she would an old piece of furniture inherited from the Electress, or else to banish him forthwith.

The Electress's death was the worst blow that could have befallen Leibniz, for it was to his friendship with her that he owed such standing as he had at a Court where, because of his many uncompleted projects and his abortive undertakings, he was not highly regarded. Soon after her death he had a taste of what was in store for him, for on returning from Vienna he was forbidden to travel. By this edict George I hoped to force him to complete his work on the history of the House of Guelph. It must be remembered that the efforts Leibniz had made to secure the crown of England for the House of Hanover were very much under-estimated. But it would not be right to measure Leibniz's political effectiveness by the yardstick of Electoral policy. The Elector's aloofness on the question of the succession sprang more from a lack of interest than from political conviction or insight. There were many plans afoot to win England for Hanover. Some of these, though well-intentioned, actually jeopardized Hanover's just claims. Practically no importance can be attached to the various memoranda on the subject. The eventual success of the claim was due in large part to Leibniz's inexhaustible energy, but in all that he did his characteristic method of working anonymously under the aegis of others produced the usual bad impression. A human weakness is revealed here, an uncertainty typical of the man, which was also a consequence of his anomalous semi-official, semi-private position in George's entourage.

Near Leibniz lived another famous contemporary, Handel, for whom, it is true, Hanover was merely a stepping-stone on his way to England. He first came to the town from Italy in 1709, on the invitation of Prince Ernest. It was thought that he might succeed Agostino Steffani (1654–1728), the highly-esteemed Court Director of Music. But restlessness soon drove him further afield. He first visited England in 1710, a risky proceeding, for he had not sought leave of absence from his Hanoverian master, who, by one of the strangest paradoxes in the history of music, was to follow him across the Channel four years later to ascend the vacant throne of England, and was to prove a right royal patron in the country of their adoption. In the interval the composer had made such a name for himself with a 'Te Deum' composed for the signing of the Treaty of Utrecht in 1713 that Queen Anne had provided him with a pension, not inconsiderable for that time, of £200. On the arrival of George I there seemed at first a certain coolness in his relations with Handel, but it was soon apparent that the King was truly pleased to see his errant musician again, and bore him no grudge for his unauthorized departure from Hanover.

Steffani was not the only Italian at the Court of Hanover. With him were divers other adventurous and mysterious characters, many of dubious origin, who had come into contact with the Hanoverian Dukes during the latters' regular visits to Italy. Their titles in some cases were as spurious as the academic honours they laid claim to; but this did not prevent them trading on both in their bid for public attention. Typical of the prevailing admiration for all things foreign was the unlimited esteem these sometimes quite unworthy persons enjoyed at Court. They were welcomed as amusing gossips, as inspired extemporizers. As musicians, singers, librettists, painters, masons, and workers in stucco, they made themselves useful and thus indispensable. Up to about 1700 the Italians ruled the musical life of Hanover. They did not do badly out of it; many of them held comparatively important positions in the small baroque Courts of other North German princes. Steffani embodied the culturally stimulating element brought in by the Italians. Another, more nefarious, element was represented by Count Montalban, representative of a less inspiring circle, and heavily compromised in the Königsmarck affair.

In the capital the theatre played a special rôle. In sympathy with the taste of the time the French theatre naturally prevailed. It must be remembered that the French baroque theatre in Hanover was the first of its kind in all Germany, and enjoyed the longest life. Hanover acquired its first play-house in 1668, when the Duke built a small Court Theatre in the Leineschloss, his Palace there. Before that, per-formances had been given in the ballroom. But one theatre was not enough, and in 1689 an Opera House was opened in the town. Even that was not sufficient, and the actors soon had a third stage at their disposal, the 'Hecken-theater', an open-air stage in the castle gardens at Herren-hausen. This has been restored, and plays are now regularly performed there in the summer months.

With the erection of the Orangery at Herrenhausen, where a stage was constructed in the Gallery, further opportunities were available for theatrical performances. In addition there was the theatre in the Duke's hunting lodge at Göhrde. Although performances in the 'Hecken-theater' in Herrenhausen were possible only in fine weather, and the Court spent only a few weeks in the autumn at Göhrde, while performances were not given regularly in the Orangery and Gallery, there were nevertheless in the Electorate of Hanover no less than six places where plays could be staged. This speaks well for the cultural pro-clivities of her rulers, and leads us to conclude that the Court could appreciate good drama. Indeed, the Court delighted in theatrical entertainment, and the fact that provision was made for a theatre in the plans for the royal residence in Hanover confirms the official character of the Court players and their cultural importance. The Elector himself was the chief 'Theaterdirektor'. The control of artistic affairs was no doubt in the hands of the ablest actor, but the final decision as to choice of play or dates of performance rested with the Elector. He could almost be called the stage manager. It is apparent that he felt responsible for his theatre, and went out of his way to care for individual actors, and to concern himself with their personal affairs. This provision by the Guelph rulers of a Court Theatre on the French model makes it clear that the Hanoverian Court was important not only politically but also culturally, for it possessed a permanent theatre such as few German capitals could boast of at that time.

It was the high reputation of this Court Theatre that had lured Agostino Steffani to Hanover from the Court of the Elector of Bavaria. He also proved useful in affairs of state, and came forward as a spokesman for the ninth Electorate. Moreover, it was through him and Count Kielmannsegge that George Louis became acquainted with Handel.

George Louis loved to hear his Court at Herrenhausen compared to that at Dresden. There was the same display of pomp, the same etiquette, the same abundance of courtiers, and of beautiful, frivolous women, the same ostentation covering a hidden poverty and squalor. A commentator wrote:

> There existed in Hanover a moral law against which the excesses of undisciplined minds crumbled away. This was due to three factors: a Leibniz modestly and creatively at work there; the exclusion of the 'regiment of women' from government and politics; and finally the feminine charm of Sophia, her daughter, and her granddaughter.

A vividly-written description of the entertainments provided for the Electoral Court during Lent in the year 1702 is to be found in a letter from Leibniz to Princess Louise of Hohenzollern-Hechingen. Masquerades, balls, convivial games and plays follow one another, he wrote. A continual alternation of entertainments was planned, and since the present did not seem to offer sufficient material for diversion, they looked to the past, and enacted the stories of Petronius. The King of Prussia, the Elector, his younger brother, Ernest Augustus, and the Duchess of Kurland, who was on a visit to Herrenhausen, divided the parts among them. Only the serious-minded Electoral-Mother and George William took no share in the proceedings. *Trimalchio's Feast* provided the framework for a series of entertainments. Pages brought in pies from which, when they were opened, flew birds that had fallen victim to the fowler's snares. The donkey laden with olives was there, as were the twelve signs of the Zodiac. Falernian wine was drunk, and everyone felt at ease amid merrymaking that was formal and familiar at the same time.

Towards the end of the seventeenth century the erection of the Palace at Herrenhausen was completed under the direction of the Groom of the Bedchamber, Quirini. The faithfulness with which architect and landscape artist managed to translate the taste of Versailles into that of Calenberg was matched by the eagerness with which grandiose copies of the ideas of the blue-stockings by the Seine were reproduced on the banks of the Leine. On feast-days celebrated by the Royal House nymphs could be heard singing madrigals and sonnets near brooks and in cleverly-adapted arbours; arcadian shepherds hymned the marvels of the day in stately alexandrines. Once Ernest Augustus had achieved the Electorate, life at his Court had to be in no way inferior to that at Dresden; but the formal etiquette that obtained there was not transported to Hanover, where a freer atmosphere reigned, and visitors could bask in the natural charm and delicacy which emanated from Sophia. The background of this courtly life was French, since all luxuries came from Paris, from whence also came almost all the servants for kitchen and

wardrobe. As early as 1688 Freiherr von Platen, on a visit
to the French capital, had engaged on behalf of his master
a *maître d'hôtel*, and entrusted him with the task of bringing
to Hanover a considerable number of French servants.

Amidst the courtly splendours of Hanover and at nearby
Celle events were enacted whose pathos turned sometimes
to tragedy. For over three hundred years the castle at Celle
had been one of the residences of the Dukes of Brunswick
and Lüneburg, of whom not one is remembered today in
spite of their proved political ability. Among them were
such men as the 'seven Guelph brothers', who spared their
people the disorders which might have arisen over the
succession by deciding to draw lots to determine which
one of them should be the only one to marry according to
his rank. After each had ruled in turn, the last brother
left the Duchy to the children of the man chosen by lot.
At the time this arrangement caused a sensation in Europe,
and the Sultan of Turkey is said to have declared his desire
to visit Celle and see for himself this miracle of reason and
brotherly love. Today the brothers are forgotten, but the
destinies of three royal ladies whose lives were intimately
associated with the castle at Celle — Eléonor d'Olbreuse,
Sophia Dorothea and Caroline Mathilda — still have
power to arouse a passionate interest. Many European
historians, dramatists and writers have found inspiration
in their lives and loves. The usual human curiosity about
Court circles is not enough to explain the lasting fascina-
tion of the fates of these three women, whose heart-felt
tragedies have survived the passage of time.

Eléonor d'Olbreuse (1639–1722), a beautiful, vivacious
French Huguenot descended from the lesser nobility of
Poitou, became lady-in-waiting to the Princess of Tarent,
a position in which it was easily possible for an ambitious
young woman to achieve a distinguished marriage. Eléonor

met her destiny in the person of George William of Brunswick-Lüneburg. By his contemporaries, with their rigid concepts of rank, a marriage with her would be considered beneath his dignity. However, he was in a somewhat unusual situation, and could do as he pleased. He had originally been betrothed, in 1656, to Sophia, daughter of the 'Winter King' of Bohemia and Elizabeth of England, but two years later he renounced her in favour of his younger brother Ernest Augustus, and promised in writing to spend the rest of his life 'in coelibatu', and on his death to bequeath his estates to any male heirs of the said brother. This strange arrangement no doubt delighted the prospective bridegroom, who, though the youngest of four brothers, thus received an unexpected but no less welcome stroke of good fortune, but it may have been less welcome to the bride. No one will ever know whom the Electress Sophia loved more, George William or Ernest Augustus — or whether perhaps she loved them both? How proud she was, this shrewd, plain, almost too clever Princess of an impoverished House! Although her father had reigned only one winter as King of Bohemia, her grandfather had been James I, King of England — a fact that Sophia never forgot. As she walked in her beloved garden at Herrenhausen, awaiting the outcome of the exciting events that marked the evening of her life, the crown of England seemed already within her grasp!

It was perhaps too much to ask of George William that he should keep his promise never to marry. He broke his word for love of Eléonor d'Olbreuse, probably because he could not win her by any other means. Theirs was a happy marriage, a rare event in Court circles. Because it was morganatic, Eléonor could not be Duchess of Celle officially, but as Madame de Harbourg she was included in the prayers for the royal family. Even this concession was not easily won, particularly as Eléonor's sister-in-law, Sophia, lost no opportunity of reminding her of her inferiority in rank. But Eléonor, with her dark-eyed beauty, was just what George William needed if he was to settle down, for in his youth he had differed little from the other princes of his time, and though always discreet, he had not scrupled to enjoy the prerogatives of his rank. But in the event he proved a faithful and loyal husband, championing his wife against the hostility of his censorious family until the difficulties of her position as a stranger, of inferior birth and a different religion, were smoothed away. For her sake George William gave up his trips 'incognito' to Venice; for her sake, and for his own, deprived as he was of other outlets, he spent his energies on the castle at Celle, adding baroque rooms and façades, importing actors, Italian operas and a French orchestra that eventually attracted Johann Sebastian Bach to Celle. For her sake, too, he invited numerous Frenchmen to Court. But his devotion to her never dwindled into subservience, never gave proof of that weakness that was to show itself at the time of the Revocation of the Edict of Nantes, when George William, the honest Protestant, gave way before the Catholic King Louis XIV and acquiesced in French policy. His Huguenot wife, torn between patriotism and her own religious zeal, nevertheless did not waver for a single moment in her allegiance to the Protestant cause of William of Orange, Louis XIV's inveterate opponent. George William, 'usually called the Duke of Celle' (Rousseau), could count himself fortunate in the possession of such a wife, and in a marriage which continued harmoniously until in 1694 the marriage of their only daughter ended in disaster.

This daughter, Sophia Dorothea (1666–1726), was their only child, and she was no doubt spoilt by both her parents. She spent her happiest years in the castle at Celle. As an acknowledged beauty and an heiress (the strange agreement between her father and her uncle had obviously not been taken seriously by the Courts of Europe) she was soon sought in marriage by a glittering circle of suitors. She was betrothed for the first time before she reached her tenth year, but her fiancé, a cousin from Wolfenbüttel, was killed in battle only a year later. However, offers of marriage from Denmark, Sweden, Württemberg and Bavaria followed in quick succession. All this must have filled Ernest Augustus and Sophia, away in Hanover, with the deepest suspicions. The father had already broken his promise to remain a bachelor, and it had cost him a great deal to soothe them both and to affirm his loyalty to the agreement — at least as far as the succession was concerned. But the question naturally arose, would a son-in-law and his adherents at Celle be equally ready to recognize the *status quo*? The more powerful he was, the more likely he was to disregard such an undertaking. Was it Sophia, blessed with several sons, who discovered the way out of the impasse? Was it she who decided that her eldest son should marry the Celle heiress, and so ensure the succession of the Dukedom to the Electorate of Hanover? It was a splendid solution, though perhaps a distasteful one. As she wrote: 'It is a bitter pill, but when it is gilded with 100,000 ducats, one shuts one's eyes, and swallows it!'

George William was probably quite happy about this solution which, at least indirectly, assured to his heirs the succession he had thrown away. Eléonor, who was more far-sighted, was perhaps not too happy to see her beloved only daughter married for political reasons. Nevertheless the wedding took place just before Christmas, 1688, in the castle at Celle. The issue of this unhappy union was two children, a son George, who later became George II of England, and a daughter named after her mother,

Sophia Dorothea, who was to be the unhappy Queen of Prussia, wife of the 'Soldier King' and mother of Frederick the Great. Thus it was the destiny of one of the famous women of Celle to be the ancestress of two great powers — England and Prussia.

The result of this marriage of convenience can easily be foreseen. A young soldier of fortune, Philip Christopher, Count Königsmarck, a Swede who had squandered the wealth amassed by his forebears in the Thirty Years' War, entered the service of the Elector of Hanover. It was not long before he had won the heart of the Electoral Princess. How much of his affection was genuine, how much cold calculation, is irrelevant; the letters that passed between them reveal a burning passion that made short work of all reasons of state policy, all thoughts of discretion. A catastrophe could not be averted. One summer's evening in 1694, at the instigation of the Countess von Platen, whose unrequited love for the handsome Swede twenty years her junior had turned to hate, Königsmarck, brother of Aurora the mistress of Augustus the Strong of Saxony, was murdered by Count Nicole Montalban. After his death Sophia Dorothea refused to return to the husband she did not love. The Divorce Courts declared her the guilty party, and after a short incarceration in Lauenau she was banished to Ahlden. Here she remained in barren imprisonment for thirty-two years, separated from her husband, her children and her parents. Eléonor, who had learnt the virtue of patience, paid many visits to her unhappy daughter, but her father, who had been deeply hurt by her conduct, refused to communicate with her. He had hoped, by the sacrifice of his child, to atone for the errors of his youth. When all allowances are made, the blame for Ahlden must lie at his door. Sophia Dorothea sent many letters humbly begging for forgiveness, and asking to be allowed to see her children. They remained unanswered, and she was to all intents and purposes 'dead', while her husband ruled in England as George I. Even her portraits, commissioned from the Court painters who had once pressed so gallantly, so enthusiastically, around her in former days, disappeared from the castle walls. It is only in our own time that they have been brought together again, often from collections where they were unrecognized or wrongly titled.

Fiction soon mingled with fact in retelling her story. Even during her lifetime confused accounts of her fate were in circulation. All bore the obvious imprint of the gossip-monger; only her uncle, Anton Ulrich of Brunswick-Wolfenbüttel, 'Der Siegprangende' — the highly successful — the learned member of the Order of Palms of the 'Fruchtbringende Gesellschaft', an important linguistic and literary association of the seventeenth century, proved a reliable eye-witness. In his 7,000-page 'roman à clef' in six volumes, *The Roman Octavia*, he has drawn, indirectly, a tolerably accurate picture of her fate. The unlucky star that governed the destiny of this much-loved Princess ruled her fate after death. She died at Ahlden in 1726, and was buried wretchedly in the village churchyard there. Later her body was removed secretly, after a short ceremony, to the crypt of the church in Celle by a zealous schoolmaster and a pastor, who were rewarded for this kindly deed by her son George II. Finally, in the present century, thieves broke open her coffin in a vain search for the jewels that were not there.

The third royal lady of Celle, Caroline Matilda (1751–1775), sister of George III of England, was married at the age of fifteen to Christian VII of Denmark. Like Sophia Dorothea's, this was another political alliance; like hers it was an unhappy one. The wife was young and immature, the husband already an invalid, destined soon to die insane. Misfortune was bound to ensue. It was brought about by Johann Friedrich Struensee (1737–72), an ambitious and not untalented German doctor who had gained the confidence of the Danish king. He was the only man near the Throne, a freethinker and a reformer, an ardent disciple of Rousseau and the French *philosophes*. Profiting by the growing insanity of Christian VII he became sole minister and virtual ruler of Denmark. After a period of initial mistrust Caroline Matilda became his most ardent admirer. That she was also his mistress was firmly believed by her contemporaries, and even her brother could hardly have doubted it. Nemesis soon overtook the guilty pair. Juliana Maria, the Danish Dowager Queen, mother of Christian VII, had Struensee arrested in 1772, after a Court Ball. Fearing for his life, Struensee betrayed the Queen who, in the hope of saving him, pleaded his cause up to the last; but all in vain. He was tried, condemned and executed, the sentence reading 'that Johann Friedrich Struensee's right hand, and thereafter his head, be struck off, his body quartered and placed on the wheel, his hand and head impaled upon a stake.' After Struensee's death the Queen, whose husband had divorced her, was severely threatened. This roused the fury of the English, who felt that, guilty or not, she had already been sufficiently punished. George III's fleet lay ready to attack, but the Danes hurriedly, and, one presumes, not unwillingly, delivered the Queen safely aboard an English ship. George III appointed as his sister's residence the castle at Celle. His brother-in-law, a prince of Mecklenburg-Strelitz, was in command there, and the whole city turned out to greet the tragic queen with genuine enthusiasm. Their affection was returned, and Caroline Matilda stayed peacefully in Celle for the next two years, dying at the age of twenty-five. It was a period of peace and reconciliation. After her death Goethe's drawing-master designed the memorial placed in the French garden where she had loved to spend her time. Her place in the Cathedral of Roskilde, where the Kings and Queens of Denmark lie at rest, remains empty. She was buried far away, in the crypt of the church at Celle, near Eléonor d'Olbreuse and Sophia Dorothea. Of the three coffins, hers is the only one to be richly decorated.

At the beginning of the eighteenth century the Electorate of Hanover measured 500 square miles and had about 750,000 inhabitants. It comprised the dukedoms of Calenberg and Lüneburg, the principalities of Göttingen and Grubenhagen, the counties of Hoya and Diepholz, and the dukedom of Saxony-Lauenburg, to which were later added the bishoprics of Bremen and Verden that Sweden had acquired by the Peace of Westphalia and later sold to Hanover. The Electorate was known throughout the Empire for its natural resources. The rich mineral deposits in the Harz mountains greatly helped in making Hanover prosperous. The first silver mines in Europe were discovered in the Harz in the year 968. Iron, copper, lead, zinc and sulphur had been mined in Hanover since time immemorial. The transportation of goods was made easy by the favourable position of the rivers Elbe, Weser, Aller and Ems. At the same time, in neighbouring Brunswick, the wool and linen industries thrived, and these goods too were transported by river, or along the great highways that formed the trade routes from Scandinavia through Hanover to the south. This provided the Elector with a considerable income, which in turn enabled him not only to keep a standing army of 18,000 men from amongst his own subjects, but also to employ another army of 14,000 mercenaries. It is easy to understand why the Emperor Leopold I thought it worth an Elector's Hat to have this force at his disposal! In 1737 a university was founded at Göttingen which was to develop rapidly into an intellectual centre for North Germany.

The Hanoverians were a prosperous people, loyal to the Electoral House, which ruled them patriarchally in the best sense of the word. Up to the conquest of the country by Napoleon in 1803, neither the organization of government nor the constitution suffered any real change. With a tenacity inherited from Lower Saxony, the Hanoverians opposed all innovations with antipathy and an indomitable mistrust. It was this conservative outlook that brought upon them the frequent scorn and censure of their contemporaries. Their Government, which was called 'ces maudites perruques d'Hannovre' by Frederick II of Prussia, and the 'European Chinese' by Freiherr vom Stein, presided over a narrow-minded society, at variance with the enlightened spirit of the times. As for the Court, it was witty and brilliant in the extravagant baroque manner. John Toland, on the occasion of his visit in 1702, described it as 'extremely polite and well accounted, even in Germany, as the best for Civility and Decorum.' However superficial this judgment may sound, there was something charming and peaceful about Hanover, so that one can easily understand why the first two Guelph Kings longed, in the noisy metropolis of London, for the tranquillity of Herrenhausen.

As Elector of Hanover, the King of England exercised absolute power, and no decisions could be taken in civil or military matters without his approval. He appointed and dismissed ministers at his own discretion; he was Commander-in-Chief of the Hanoverian army, and dictated the course of foreign policy. Hanover was a typical small German State, perhaps better governed than some, prosperous and comparatively peace-loving. Here the Elector could say, with perhaps more truth than Louis XIV: 'L'Etat, c'est moi!' George I did not leave Hanover willingly. He went back as often as he could, and was buried there. Hanover mourned for many years his removal to London. The people were not elated by their Prince's elevation to the throne of England, nor were they consoled by the fame this honour brought them. It was not so much the loss suffered by the departure of the Court that made them unhappy as the fact that their ruler was leaving the country. By virtue of their mentality, these North Germans were slow to adapt themselves to innovations. The splendour that illuminated the throne of the Guelph Kings in England reflected, it is true, a little glory upon the land of their birth, particularly when they visited it. But in the course of time it was inevitable that they should drift further and further away from the Electorate. The bond between the Prince and his people was loosened, and succeeding generations of the Royal House were to become completely British in manners and outlook. Many of his subjects may have had a premonition of this as they watched George Louis depart.

The various regions which made up the Electorate were traditionally represented in the provincial Estates; but even after his accession it would never have occurred to the Guelph ruler to set up in Hanover a parliamentary government on the English model. The Estates, made up of knights, bishops, and rich citizens, and substantial farmers flattered themselves on their local autonomy, but this was only a pleasing fiction. In reality, the Electorate was governed from Hanover, by ministers responsible only to the Elector, who himself had charge of home and foreign policy. His was a paternal despotism over subjects who gave no cause for anxiety, but showed a blind loyalty to their ruler, and would never venture to criticize him or the measures he took. The foreign interests of the Electorate were limited almost exclusively to North-East Germany, particularly to its powerful neighbours Brandenburg-Prussia, and the Baltic States, Sweden, Denmark, and Russia, so closely allied by marriage to the ruling Houses of Mecklenburg, Anhalt and Holstein. Otherwise the new 'arch-treasurer of the Empire' — George Louis received this title in 1710 as a reward for loyal service to the Emperor Joseph I — concerned himself exclusively with his feudal overlord, the Emperor. For example, in gratitude for his elevation to the Electorate he went to great trouble to secure Imperial approval for the purchase of Bremen and Verden.

Even during his absence in England the Elector maintained direct control over military matters in Hanover, and did not appoint a representative to deal with them. In civil matters, the ministers who had stayed behind had to keep the King continually informed of what was happening. Each king in turn maintained his right to sign personally all amnesties, and to give permission for the judicial prosecution of any highly-placed Hanoverian. In foreign affairs, ministers were only allowed to act independently in time of national emergency — a threatened invasion, for instance. Hanoverian diplomats abroad had to send duplicates of their communications to London. No minister in Hanover had the authority to sanction expenditure of more than 50 thalers without the King's permission. The ministers were allowed to choose only their own secretaries; all other appointments were made arbitrarily from London. Throughout the period 1714–1837, a Hanoverian Ambassador was accredited to the Court of St James's in addition to a Hanoverian Minister with two secretaries in London. These formed the German Chancery, and it was through them that the Electoral decrees were transmitted.

It is interesting to note that George I and his first two successors wore the English Crown as Electors, but as Kings of England they never used their Electoral title. It would perhaps be true to say that Hanover was considered in Great Britain as a foreign power. For the Elector himself, however, it remained his pleasant private realm, with its congenial capital, its charming summer residence at Göhrde, and the pleasures of hunting in its fine forests. In Hanover there were no pinpricks from an obstinate parliament to irritate him, but only a pleasant relationship with a people who looked upon their ruler as a patriarch, and believed he knew how to order all things for the best.

For a long time historians have given a one-sided view of the Hanoverian Kings of England; some have sharply condemned them. Thackeray was largely responsible for establishing this erroneous picture when he asserted 'in all things George I thought only of Hanover. He plundered, and so did his household. George II had neither morals nor wit, but despite the fact he was no worse than other monarchs of his time.' This says much for the novelist, but little for the historian! In his lectures on the Personal Union, A. W. Ward (1837–1924) worked assiduously to reinstate George I, and to settle the question as to whether England or Hanover suffered most in the end through the union. For us, the last word on the subject has been written by Dr J. H. Plumb in his excellent book *The First Four Georges*. In judging George I today we must not underestimate his shrewd restraint in the matter of English Cabinet politics. A further argument in his favour can be found in the strengthening of the Constitution brought about by his strict observance of its principles. This, together with the peace he assured for England, and the knowledge of human nature that made him appoint such men as Stanhope and Walpole as ministers, is the salient factor to be kept in mind in an attempt to assess the man who came from a petty principality of Germany to rule over England. As to whether England's interests were prejudiced by a predominating consideration for Hanover, it must suffice to quote Bolingbroke, who assuredly was no admirer of his new master. In November, 1741, he wrote in a letter to Lyttelton that 'it would be wrong to make any such assertion'. One cannot say with confidence that a deliberate preference was shown towards Hanover. On the other hand, a certain natural inclination to protect one's own property against the threats of a European coalition is only too understandable. The most we can say is that in the long run it did Great Britain no harm.

SUGGESTIONS FOR FURTHER READING

Thornton, P. M., *The Brunswick Accession*, Ridgway, 1887.

Wilkins, W. H., *The Love of an Uncrowned Queen*, Hutchinson, 1900.

Ward, A. W., *The Electress Sophia and the Hanoverian Succession*, Goupil, 1903.

Baily, F. E., *Sophia of Hanover and her Times*, Hutchinson, 1936.

Thackeray, W. M., *The English Humourists*; *The Four Georges*; Falcon Press, 1948.

Toland, J., *The Elegy and Character of Her Royal Highness the late Princess Sophia*.

Plumb, J. H., *The First Four Georges*, Batsford, 1956.

The Electress Sophia of Hanover, *Memoirs*.

Baron von Pöllnitz, *Memoirs*.

Havemann, W., *Geschichte von Braunschweig und Hannover*.

von Heinemann, O., *Geschichte der Lande Braunschweig und Lüneburg*.

Rosendahl, E., *Geschichte Niedersachsens im Spiegel der Reichsgeschichte.*

Michael, W., *Englische Geschichte im Achtzehnten Jahrhundert*, (translated and adapted from the German: *England under George I*, Macmillan, 1936).

PRINTED IN GREAT BRITAIN
BY ROBERT MACLEHOSE AND CO. LTD
THE UNIVERSITY PRESS, GLASGOW